Holy Purpose

LUTHERAN VOICES

Holy Purpose
The Blessings of Service, Obedience, and Faith

Carolyn Coon Mowchan

Augsburg Fortress

Minneapolis

HOLY PURPOSE
The Blessings of Service, Obedience, and Faith

Large-quantity purchases or custom editions of this book are available at a discount from the publisher. For more information, contact the sales department at Augsburg Fortress, Publishers, 1-800-328-4648, or write to: Sales Director, Augsburg Fortress, Publishers, Box 1209, Minneapolis, MN 55440-1209.

Library of Congress Cataloging-in-Publication Data
Mowchan, Carolyn.
  Holy purpose : the blessings of service, obedience, and faith / by Carolyn Coon Mowchan.
      p. cm. — (Lutheran voices series)
  Includes bibliographical references.
  ISBN-13: 978-0-8066-5333-4 (pbk. : alk. paper)
  1. Christian life—Lutheran authors. I. Title.
  BV4501.3.M69 2007
    248.4'841—dc22   2006100733

11   10   09   08   07   1   2   3   4   5   6   7   8   9   10

For my husband and my daughters
who have taught me so much about the joy of abundant life!

And for the people of Trinity Lutheran Church
in Spooner, Wisconsin,
who have honored me with their trust
and who have been wonderful companions for the journey!

And for God, who never gives up on us.

Contents

Preface

I guess I never completely gave up on my Southern upbringing that taught me a relationship with God and Jesus was intimate and personal, not just moral and intellectual. As a Southern migrant from the heat of being a Baptist to the relief of being a Lutheran, I have wrestled for a long time with issues now dividing Christians. What is a personal relationship with Jesus? Where do we meet the risen Lord? Is faith about feelings or good order and right doctrine? Where is God transforming lives in our focus on inter-church relationships, social justice, and denominational self-preservation? Where is God breaking hearts and healing sorrow in the midst of struggles about new hymnals, correct worship, and holy tradition? I've often wondered why people, including myself, have so little spiritual fruit to show for what looks like a well-tended spiritual garden. I've wondered why people can be so lukewarm about faith, and how people can just walk away from the church. They are, you know. Since the 1960s all mainline protestant denominations have experienced slow and steady decline.

What I offer here in this book is some middle ground perspective on God's "plan" and "purpose" for your life, what God might be using to get your attention at the moment, and how you can let God's power heal and transform you. I'm hoping that if Martin Luther could read this he could stand it, or at least say, "I could stand here, too."

—Carolyn Mowchan

Introduction

Now that I'm finished, if I could re-title this book it would be: *The Promise: A Field Guide for God Watching.* I would then paint a picture of many people in bird watching gear standing on a hill. Some are looking through binoculars and pointing excitedly. Some are kneeling in reverence and prayer. Some are running away in terror. And some are trying to see, looking rather confused and disappointed. You can put your face on any of these figures, depending on where you are right now in your relationship with God. Or maybe you're sitting in the car listening to the radio, waiting for the God watchers to be finished.

Where do you see God active in the world these days? None of us has perfect spiritual vision, and that is most especially true of me! But if we don't recognize God present in our lives, maybe it's because we don't know where to look. Maybe our perception is blurred by bad ideas about where to look, or just plain bad ideas. Bad ideas about God and in the name of God are deadly. Ask the soldiers who died in holy wars. Ask the Jews who survived Hitler. Ask the people who have suffered from jihad. Ask the children whose parents seemed to be needed in heaven a little too early. Ask anyone who has been the brunt of violence and hurt inflicted in the name of religious truth.

Here are some untrue, powerful, but destructive spiritual ideas that are commonly accepted as truth these days: You don't need a church to be a Christian. God no longer does miracles. There's no such thing as a power of evil called "Satan." If there is a heaven, everybody gets to go. You can worship God in the woods just as faithfully as you can in a church. The difference between a true and untrue idea is whether or not it's biblical. That's why we desperately need to read the Bible!

Or maybe I would call the book: *Holy Purpose: The Bigger Picture.* Lots of us read Rick Warren's *The Purpose Driven Life* (Zondervan, 2002). Lots of us got a lot out of it and found it really inspirational. But something kept nagging at me in the back of my mind as I read it. Maybe it just stirred up something that's been surfacing in me for quite awhile. I liked the opening line of *The Purpose Driven Life:* "It's not about you." True. But I believe it also isn't just about God.

Our American ears love to be told that we are unique and special and set apart from others. I'd love to believe that God had a plan for me before I was born, and that everything that's happened to me is part of that plan. But it just doesn't hold up. I know how many times I've taken detours that weren't in God's plans. I know how much violence, death, and destruction there is. That also isn't in God's plan. We know that we have some power and control, and yet we say God is in control. We know that evil has some power. So far that's a three-way-power split: ours, God's, and the power of evil.

Finally, that's essentially what this book is about—God's part and our response. How does God use power? What can we trust God to do? I've heard what God wants and expects from me since I was old enough to be told right from wrong. But I haven't heard so much about God's end of things—at least not a lot that seems to be happening in the present. In the beginning God created and God will greet us in the end—but what's God doing right now? Is God campaigning for political parties, condemning social policies, busy working undercover so no one knows the Holy One is present? What doesn't God do? Isn't that as important as what God does?

Once we get at the heart of these questions, a new one pops up: How can we as Christians tell others about God working in our lives? For the past couple of decades Christianity has been increasingly optional, among both old and young. For the past couple of decades the Lutheran church has been shrinking rather than growing. This will only scare you if you care about the future of the church and God's mission in the world. I do. And I'm scared. Over the years I have met lots and lots of people who don't believe in God. I think that they don't believe in God because we, the church, haven't given them enough help to look for God in their own life stories. We haven't helped them ask the questions: What is God doing? How do you know? We seem to have lost discernment traditions from our Catholic origins. Somehow faith practices, along with sins, have been washed away by grace.

There are at least a couple of ways to evaluate our current understanding of what it means to be Christian. One is to ask if it works? Are people being shaped into the holy priesthood of all believers that Christ intended? Are you? Another way to evaluate it is to ask: Is it biblical? I know personal interpretation of Scripture is just that, so I invite you to check out my assumptions by keeping a Bible handy while you read this. I think God promised more than stern religious endurance, melancholy liturgies, and an easy conscience in a world that is increasingly both pagan and full of pain. What God did in both the Old and New Testament, God still does. Let's look at that and see if it can give us the confidence to point to what God is doing in our lives, now.

If the way you are currently practicing Christianity isn't making you a better and more joyful person, it's not working and it's not biblical. Jesus prayed for us so that we would have joy (John 17:13). That's my prayer for you as well. I hope this helps.

Part One

Where Have You Seen God Lately?

"Don't believe everything you think."
—carved on a stone in Seattle

"Open our eyes, Lord. We want to see Jesus."
—Bob Cull

"No one can say 'Jesus is Lord' except by the Holy Spirit."
—1 Corinthians 12:3

1

The Search

"I am the Lord, I have called you in righteousness, I have taken you by the hand and kept you; I have given you as a covenant to the people, a light to the nations, to open the eyes that are blind, to bring out the prisoners from the dungeon, from the prison those who sit in darkness. I am the Lord, that is my name" (Isa. 42:6-8a).

Picking up the Lutheran Binoculars: Grace and Faith

If you could pick up holy binoculars right now to look for God's Spirit, where would you point them? If someone grabbed a pair and looked into your life, what would they see? If you're lucky God starts leaving clues to prod you to move from thinking about religion to actually seeking God. It's not as difficult as the hide-and-seek games I played as a kid. And if we seek, God promises that we will find (Luke 11:9).

Lutherans and all Christians believe that Jesus is Lord. Christians who happen to be Lutheran also believe, among others things, that we share some understandings about how to use the Bible, what it means to be a follower of Christ, and that we expect God's love and power to change us. However you understand the process, letting Jesus be Lord is an active, daily practice that changes us from the inside out. Dare I use "choose" in a Lutheran book? Letting Jesus *be* Lord is a conscious choice. It is not at all the same thing as believing that Jesus *is* Lord. While I know that it's cold outside now, I won't experience the cold until I go outside. While I believe that God is real, I don't experience God in the present unless I attempt communication with God.

Lord, CEO, Boss—How Do We Let Jesus Lead?

Church words carry shadows from a lot of different centuries. Like a glacier moving slowly through time, Christianity has picked up and incorporated bits and pieces from every century that it has passed through. The word *Lord* is no longer in frequent use, at least at my house. So even one of the primary titles we give God can be mysterious and rather musty. I have a theater closet in my brain where I have packed away a lot of medieval props from spending time with Shakespeare. It's not hard for me to set the word *Lord* in the middle of these trappings. I imagine an elaborate setting with kings and queens in beautiful (and uncomfortable) costumes, a royal robe, scepter, and a throne room filled with the lords and ladies of the kingdom. The knights would be offering the king (or queen) their swords, while kneeling at the throne. Kneeling is obviously a gesture of surrender and submission; the sword means personal power and strength. Did you know that the practice of kneeling with bowed heads comes from the medieval practice of baring your neck for the king to chop it off if he chose? The image is of absolute vulnerability!

Step into this picture and see what it might look like to let Jesus be Lord. We submit and surrender, pledging allegiance at the feet of the king. We put at the king's service our strength, power, gifts, and resources. The king expects our service, loyalty, and willingness to sacrifice if necessary, for the good of the kingdom. The king's enemies become our enemies. The king's friends become our friends. In return we get a place at the banquet table, the affection and protection of the king, and a cool costume—the "armor of righteousness." The king becomes provider and protector. That's covenant, or pledge language: "You will be my people, and I will be your God." It's a refrain you hear over and over in the Old Testament.

So let's mix the imagery. Start trading the medieval props for contemporary equivalents. Consider this: We kneel at the throne and offer the king our Blackberries and PDAs, our checkbooks and charge cards. That gets a little closer to home. Now there are those who insist that the king takes these and begins to give detailed instructions, even commands, about what to do next. Going a step further, there are those who think that the king made arrangements for and about us before we were born. Think of it a bit like parents who set up an arranged marriage without the child's consent. As long as the child is obedient (meaning duty is more important than happiness and personal choice), life is good. Is this what we mean when we say, "God is in control" or "God has a plan"? Is the way we think of this God/king living in some mysterious place allowing for any use of our God-gifted brain and individual choice? Or is there a wizard in the basement of the castle stirring up potions and spells and directing our every step? Can we refuse the plan?

We do have that freedom. We have so much freedom that some of us can't even find the "throne room." The inability to step into a receptive attitude where we can comprehend the presence of God may be at the heart of the declining interest in Christianity. It seems to me that a lot of people live as if the old castles where the divine royalty used to live are now empty. So they stop showing up at church. This is poor theology, but seems to me to be an accurate assessment of contemporary thinking. We still admire God's handiwork, from castles to trees, but we no longer live expecting God, the potter or the architect, to show up.

In the theater, when the house lights go dark and the stage lights come up, the audience enters into an unspoken contract with the players. It's called the "suspension of disbelief." We put aside the fact that we know we are being told a story that is not really happening. The players are pretending. While we suspend our disbelief we are open to hearing or learning or even experiencing the "truth" of the story. We don't get bogged down on the missed lines, or the rough edges of the performance—the main thing is "the play" as Shakespeare said. Reading the Bible is like that. If we want to know who it is that needs to sit in that now empty throne as Lord of our lives, we need to go back to the script for clues about the role God expected Jesus to play, not just in history, but in our lives. The script is, of course, Scripture. Let's search the ancient words for what God promised us. Most of us know, if we've paid attention at all, what God expects from us. But what do we expect from God? Where did God promise to show up? Where does God still show up? How do we experience God's power and providence?

The Story Begins—Lights Up on the Servant at Center Stage

"See, the former things have come to pass, and new things I now declare; before they spring forth, I tell you of them" (Isa. 42:9).

Here's the situation: God created a good and perfect world (see Genesis 1). We now understand that without God there can be no paradise. This side of Eden there is precious little perfection. There's a snake in every garden, ants at every picnic, and somehow many of God, the potter's, human pots ended up cracked. Those would be us.

The Old Testament tells the story of God trying to repair the cracks from a distance. God spoke through prophets and kings. God made bargains, dished out punishment, blessed and anguished over the people of Israel. The covenants or contracts were made by God, broken by the people, and recorded in what became the "older testament." Moses handed down God's covenant on Mt. Sinai (see the Book of Exodus). God's part was written in stone. Our agreement must have been signed on a sticky note. Most of the books of the Old Testament tell us the story of people trying to live out or get out of the Ten Commandments. Hundreds of years before Christ, it was clear that God needed something besides the Law to shape human hearts and behavior. That's an overview of centuries of warfare, rebellion, and darkness. These were the times when God tried to force Israel into submission with mighty displays of power, punishment, and deliverance. It didn't work.

"In those days John the Baptist appeared in the wilderness of Judea, proclaiming, 'Repent, for the kingdom of heaven has come near.' This is the one of whom the prophet Isaiah spoke when he said, 'The voice of one crying out in the wilderness: Prepare the way of the Lord, make his paths straight'"(Matt. 3:3).

Since communication from a distance didn't work, even with a few plagues, locusts, and burning bushes, it was time for God to do something new. I think of it like this: We had an old, rather large car when I was a kid. I remember that when we took long family road trips there was a good bit of chaos in the back seat where we three kids were expected to be seen very little and not heard much either. Most of the time, of course, we were extremely well behaved. On those rare occasions when we weren't, we were aware that the car was a little too long for dad's arm to reach from the front seat to the back. We often doubted the sincerity of his threats, but we did quiet down a bit when he began to say, "Don't make me stop the car and come back there." "Do I have to come back there?" "Do you *want* me to come back there?" For the most part, John the Baptist picked up that tone with "shape-up-quick-God-is-getting-ready-to-come-down-here" speeches in the wilderness. Both he and my father could strike fear into the hearts of those who knew they needed to change.

Imagine Israel's incredulity when Jesus came with grace, gentleness, mercy, and compassion. That would have been as unbelievable as my father coming into the back seat and asking quietly, "Would you like an ice cream cone?" When you know you are guilty, you can hope for grace, but it's the last thing you really expect. Our expectations definitely shape our perceptions. What we expect is often what we see, whether it's there or not. So Israel for the most part didn't recognize the Messiah.

God's Promises and Priorities

So the Lord came down. And I love it that God began promising this arrival to the people of Israel long before it happened. "The idols can't do that," God said. "See if they can predict the future. Who is really God around here—you, me, or pieces of iron?" So Isaiah announced God's promise that they would once again be delivered out of slavery. No, it wasn't Moses leading the people out of Egypt—although it was a similar story. This time it was freeing the people from slavery in Babylon. (Same story, different generation.)

If you read through some of the Old Testament stories you often see that God said in essence: See, I am the one true God—more powerful than any idol, more present than any god with a small "g"—but not necessarily faster than a speeding bullet. When we ask God to show up, it's usually not on our time schedule. It took about five hundred years for Jesus to show up in Bethlehem.

Looking back at our script from Isaiah, we see that the central character of history will soon enter. His opening words will be a speech from Isaiah 61. We continue to be doubtful when people claim to have experienced God today. If anyone claimed to *be* God today, I'm sure at least the media would hold another crucifixion. We can understand the resistance from both then and now. So the stage is set with Isaiah announcing, "You have forgotten the Lord, your Maker, who stretched out the heavens and laid the foundations of all the earth. You fear continually all day long because of the fury of the oppressor, who is bent on destruction" (Isa. 51:13).

We don't know yet in what century the play is set when the lights come up. But we do know that this is an "everyman" and "everywoman" story. All of us, at one time or another, might be in need of hearing, "You have forgotten the Lord." Let those without fear, anxiety, and sin cast the first stones. Get ready to take off your shoes because I think I can help us find some holy ground.

God's priorities haven't changed. Chances are if you find places in your corner of the world where the promises from Isaiah are coming true, if you have any spiritual radar at all, you will be able to detect God in the world and the Spirit at work. Look where God's existence and power have made a difference and God's wisdom (the Bible) is respected, where people are given strength beyond their own human limits, where hope for deliverance from pain and failure is reborn and a broken relationship with God is restored. Look where people live with inner peace, compassion, and a sense of responsibility for others. Look where people are given trust in God, strength, hope, and the freedom to make necessary changes.

For Group Discussion and/or Personal Reflection

1. How do you understand the Old Testament and the New Testament fitting together?

2. What are some modern idols? What do people want from these things? What are they willing to give up for them? How would you compare the power we give our modern idols to expectations we have about God? Why is it so difficult to trust God?

3. Where have you seen or experienced glimpses of God's power at work in the world? In your personal life? How has it changed you?

2

Truth and Good Judgment

"You are my witnesses, says the Lord, and my servant whom I have chosen, so that you may know and believe me and understand that I am he. Before me no god was formed, nor shall there be any after me" (Isa. 43:10).

"Here is my servant, whom I uphold, my chosen, in whom my soul delights; I have put my spirit upon him; he will bring forth justice to the nations" (Isa. 42:1).

The Servant Enters

Here he is. The grand entrance of the promised servant was announced with all the heavenly fanfare the angels could muster. Even though they were singing to rather unlikely witnesses, the shepherds got the message: "To you is born this day . . ." (Luke 2:15 ff). Something from beyond the earth stepped into our history.

When the holy pulls back the veil (Mark 15:38) and is clearly visible upon the earth, biblically it seems always to be centered on one purpose: to demonstrate the reality of God's existence. The burning bush didn't burn because the bush needed it; Moses needed to know that God was speaking. The Red Sea didn't part because of a freak weather system; the people of Israel needed to know that God was leading. The angels didn't sing to the shepherds because the anthem they had been rehearsing since who knows when was finally ready. Miracles and glimpses of God's strength and power have one purpose: to make visible the reality of God, the fact that God exists, cares, and acts. Unfortunately, the trouble with miracles, like feeding bread and fish to the crowd of five thousand, is that they don't always elicit the response God intended. Like children watching magic tricks, the response is often, "Do another one!" So the crowd who ate loaves and fish were amazed, and then they wanted dessert. "Let's make him king and keep the food coming!" (John 6:15).

God still demonstrates supernatural power to make contact with us. God still wants us to live in harmonious relationship with each other and with our Creator. Our human nature since the beginning of time is often called "sinful" because we keep walking away from relationships with each other and with God. We consistently make poor choices. The word *justice* in Hebrew implies judgment as in "good judgment," as well as fairness. God wants to deliver us from evil and pain and prevent us from doing harm.

Mission Number One: Communication

"For thus says the Lord, who created the heavens (he is God!), who formed the earth and made it (he established it; he did not create it a chaos, he formed it to be inhabited!): I am the Lord, and there is no other. I did not speak in secret, in a land of darkness; I did not say to the offspring of Jacob, 'Seek me in chaos.' I the Lord speak the truth, I declare what is right" (Isa. 45:18-19).

There are parts of Isaiah that describe the work of a mysterious "servant." Traditionally, Christians have assumed this to be Jesus. He was the "something new" that God promised. He was the one coming to deliver, to redeem, to save. Not only would he preach good news, he *was* good news. He was God's Word, God's statement, God's grand entrance and "tah-dah."—"In the beginning was the Word, and the Word was with God, and the Word was God" (John 1:1).

When Jesus opened the scroll in the temple and read his first public words of ministry, they communicated who he was and who had sent him. He read from the prophet Isaiah: "The spirit of the

Lord God is upon me, because the Lord has anointed me; he has sent me to bring good news to the oppressed, to bind up the brokenhearted, to proclaim liberty to the captives, and release to the prisoners; to proclaim the year of the Lord's favor, and the day of vengeance of our God; to comfort all who mourn; to provide for those who mourn in Zion—to give them a garland instead of ashes, the oil of gladness instead of mourning, the mantle of praise instead of a faint spirit. They will be called oaks of righteousness, the planting of the Lord, to display his glory" (Isa. 61:1-3).

The servant was sent to communicate God's purpose for God's people. Isaiah's language is some of the most beautiful in Scripture. It is poetic and inspiring: "The leopard shall lie down with the kid" (Isa. 11:6), "How beautiful upon the mountains are the feet of the messenger who announces peace" (Isa. 52:7). However, we sometimes have difficulty understanding anything beyond the poetic imagery. Should we look for the presence of God in zoos or shoe stores? Seen any leopards cuddling with little goats lately? How do we know that these prophecies came true? Where do we look to see God still keeping them?

What Does This Mean?

The psalmist proclaims, "[The Lord] executes justice for the oppressed; [the Lord] gives food to the hungry. The Lord sets the prisoners free; the Lord opens the eyes of the blind" (Ps. 146:7-8). Before we can go tripping down the path of social justice, relief work, and hope for a world with no crime, punishment, or need for guide dogs and Braille, what is really being said when the word *justice* is used here? It implies more than fairness, political reform, and compassion for the less fortunate. Not that those ideals aren't important. But the Hebrew word that is used here has the same root word as that for *righteousness*, which means, "giving to those in need, what they need, out of your ability to give." If you don't believe that

God is real, why would you care about God's expectations? The first mission Jesus was given was to cure human blindness—the things that keep us from seeing God (often demonstrated by literally opening the eyes of the blind). The truth that Jesus communicated was the truth that God loves us (the Gospel) and we don't have to earn that love. The heart of that message, both by example and by verbal communication, is that as God is generous in loving us, we should be generous in sharing that gift with others. The word for *justice* also says "good judgment" and "wisdom." God's wisdom tells us that the strong have the responsibility to care for the weak. The "haves" are expected to care for the "have nots." That's God's understanding of fairness, or justice. But God asks us to be witnesses—people whose actions point to the power, reality, and love of God. We can't witness to what we haven't seen.

Releasing the captives doesn't simply mean closing down the prisons. Rather, it speaks to the way we have the capacity to put others and ourselves behind bars. Our perspective, or way of seeing, can become a small cage that cripples souls. Jesus told his disciples that they had the power to release people from their sins or leave them bound up and burdened in their past. So do we. We can withhold forgiveness and offer blame instead. We can shut our hearts to God and live in fear instead of faith. We can be hardhearted like the Pharaoh in Egypt who refused to be moved by compassion for those who suffered. We can harden our hearts and become blind to what God is doing in our lives and the lives of other people. Or we can let God's spirit change us and our perspective.

Miracles Instead of Press Releases

The first truth that people need(ed) to know about God is that the Creator is still real, powerful, present, and cares about us. Now think about the things Jesus did to demonstrate that. He had power over nature as only God does. He calmed the storm, walked on water, and turned water into wine. He could provide food. (Loaves and fishes were a step up from his father's manna.) He could heal diseases and bring people back from death. Finally he demonstrated power over death by appearing to enough people who could be credible witnesses that the word spread fairly quickly, considering their lack of media and modern technology!

Would people have believed Jesus if he hadn't been able to demonstrate supernatural powers? Would people have believed the disciples if they hadn't been able to demonstrate similar power? Even Moses got a staff, a fiery pillar, and a global positioning device to lead the people through the desert to the Promised Land. What should that tell us? When God calls us into service, God equips us with the tools we need.

Faith is shared and grown through relationships of trust. Who are the people in your life who have helped you believe the following central truths?

- God is real (historically present in the past, personally present in our times);
- God is powerful (and answers prayer);
- God communicates (and speaks to our hearts through Scripture and prayer);
- God is loving (Jesus was a peace offering of love).

If God is not present, active, and not a supernatural reality that keeps breaking into our consciousness and world, we as the church are nothing more than a historical society for nostalgic people to visit once in awhile when we are in the mood.

For Group Discussion and/or Personal Reflection

1. How do you experience the presence of God as you do God's work? Who are the people who have helped communicate God's power to you?

2. Looking back, when were the times that God has seemed closest and most real to you? What were the circumstances at that time?

3. How do you understand the Holy Spirit? God poured out the power of the Holy Spirit upon Jesus (Isa. 61:1; Matt. 3:16). If you are curious, use a concordance to see how many times you can find references to "poured out my Spirit" or "Holy Spirit" in both the Old and New Testament. Here are some biblical references about the Spirit: Gen. 1:2; Num. 27:18; Neh. 9:30; Job 32:18; Psa. 104:30; Psa. 139:7; Luke 1:35; Luke 4:18; and Acts 6:10. If you really want to see the Spirit at work, read the entire book of Acts.

3

Strength from Outside Ourselves

"And he said to me 'You are my servant, Israel, in whom I will be glorified.' But I said, 'I have labored in vain, I have spent my strength for nothing and vanity; yet surely my cause is with the Lord, and my reward with my God . . . for I am honored in the sight of the Lord, and my God has become my strength'" (Isa. 49:3-4, 5).

Strength in Our Weakness

When we are in trouble and when we are not, the question is: Does God have supernatural strength? Yes. Does God use that strength on behalf of human beings? Yes. On that level there are few who would argue. That's all we need to know to get started. If we are in need, we are told to pray. But we have to give God the freedom to respond or not, for God also has a choice. God's choice is to love us—but sometimes the way that happens may be surprising.

Isaiah was sitting on a Saturday night without a word to give his listeners on Sunday morning, bone tired and shaking his head if not his fist at God. (Okay, this is not exactly biblically accurate but is essentially the story.) He said, "I've given it all I had and it really hasn't made much difference. This work is pointless and I've wasted my life, my passion, and my words" (Isa. 49:3, paraphrased). He was weary. Today we might say "burned out."

Weary is different than being tired. Weary is what happens when you go on vacation and don't come back rested. It's a kind of soul tired you can't shake with a good night's sleep. There are as many ways to get weary as there are to get tired, but weary implies one step on the slope to hopelessness and despair, or at least to the pondering of throwing in the towel and searching the want ads for a new job or a new life. Prolonged weariness begins to cripple us emotionally, physically, and spiritually. Do you see the devil smiling when you fill up your calendar to overflowing with very little that looks like rest? I do.

God's response to Isaiah was almost too enthusiastic to be caring: "Great! I'll give you a promotion. Now instead of talking to the little nation of Israel, I'll send you to the whole world" (Isa. 49:6, paraphrased). You can just imagine Isaiah thinking, "Are you listening to me, God? Don't you hear what I'm saying? I don't want a promotion. I want to quit." Still, somehow Isaiah proclaims, "I am honored in the sight of the Lord, and my God has become my strength" (Isa. 49:5). Isaiah felt called! But like a lot of people who feel called he was also tired and discouraged. A friend said to me recently, "God doesn't call the equipped. God equips the called." I read once that God wants to give to us, but when our hands are full there's no place to put what God offers. When we stop pushing on ahead, when we just stop and ask, it's amazing the way God answers.

"For thus said the Lord God, the Holy One of Israel: In returning [to me] and rest you shall be saved; in quietness and in trust shall be your strength" (Isa. 30:15). Isaiah predicted that the servant (Jesus) would point us toward the reality of God in a variety of ways. Jesus was, among other things, the perfect model of obedience. Are we allowed to think that God responds to the prayers of those who at least strive for obedience? Over and over again God said to the people of Israel, "Come back to me and I will be your God." But when they turned their backs on God, God didn't insist or intrude.

So let's say we are weary because we forgot that God can help with even small things if we ask. Sometimes the little things pile up like dominoes and it only takes one more to crash the whole expanse. How will God sustain us? Start by asking for what you really need, as long as it is "God pleasing." You might also ask God to tell you what you really need, like planning better. God does not do anything that goes against Scripture. In other words, if God said "no" in the Bible, it's still "no." That means we have to know what's in God's Word in order to know what God does or doesn't do. God won't alter the promises in Scripture or do magic. When I was studying systematic theology years ago, I found prayer very difficult because I couldn't sort out what was God's department and what wasn't. So I would pray, "If this is the kind of thing you do, Lord. . . ." It wasn't exactly a huge leap of faith. I have an easier method these days. When I pray I think about this: If God is the same yesterday, today, and tomorrow, then God is the same in Africa as God is in America. Therefore if my prayer would sound absurd on the lips of a mother with starving children in Africa, then my prayer may sound absurd to God.

Two years ago we sent a mission team to Africa. My husband said he has never seen such joyful Christians and such generous people. They understood God's provision in ways that we can seldom know. They were so eager to demonstrate Christian gratitude that often they would give our team the only food they had for the whole day. Our team came back much more inspired by their witness than they ever anticipated.

God inspires, breathes strength into us, and sends servants to support us when we are weary. God will carry our burdens, soothe our fears, quiet our hearts—and even adults need that. But God allows us dignity. We can refuse. We can make choices. We can insist on our own way. Sometimes we have to fall flat on our faces before we are willing to ask for God's help. When we are at our weakest we might finally be ready to lean on God. We make God's glory known when our own strength has burned out like last year's fireworks. Then we can be as surprised as everybody else when we see the results of our work bring light to someone's darkness. "I can do all things through Christ who strengthens me" (Phil. 4:13). We are perhaps at our best when we are most empty, because then God has more room to work!

How Does God Strengthen Us?

Over the summer I gathered some "Lutherans" around my kitchen table and coffeepot to ask some faith questions, such as, "How have you received strength from God?" Everyone agreed that God still gives us strength when we ask for it. And the stories went in many directions. Sometimes God used people to say the right thing at the right time. Sometimes a "coincidence" resolved a very difficult issue that had been prayed over long and hard. And sometimes the quiet whisper, through a hymn or a Bible passage, stilled the heart just long enough to hear a word of hope and comfort: "Do not be afraid, I am with you. I love you and you are mine." You might be humming without realizing what the song is and then realize that the words touch you in a heightened way. Sometimes it seems that just at the right moment someone will offer a word of comfort, and at that moment the volume gets turned up (like when the commercials come on television and you push the mute button). There are subtle quiet things that carry you one day at a time until you are capable of walking on your own two feet again.

"The Lord God has given me the tongue of a teacher, that I may know how to sustain the weary with a word. Morning by morning he wakens—wakens my ear to listen as those who are taught" (Isa. 50:4). Encouraging words, true words, words of wisdom and faithfulness encourage the weary. Where do these words come from? We find them when we prayerfully read God's Word, morning by morning, and day by day. God's Word not only gives us information, it also shapes our hearts. Sometimes reading the Bible needs to be begun with the prayer, "Lord, give me ears to hear," so that the words begin to make sense. Reading the Bible is much easier using a devotional guide, and my goodness, those are available everywhere! Your pastor would be delighted to give you one. God comes to us in the power of the Holy Spirit, in the work of Scripture in our hearts, in the assistance of those who serve in Jesus' name, and always when we ask.

I recently visited the home of some longtime friends. Their home has been touched with sorrow and difficulty, like most homes. Behind closed doors they have struggled with cancer, depression, and weariness. He is a faithful servant trying to help with the renewal of the church. He meets with ongoing and often painful resistance. His wife struggles with the full impact of her husband's illness along with her own deeply repressed pain from trauma in her youth. They both are walking in the shadows of death, retirement, and change, not necessarily in any given order. I can imagine him wondering if his pastoral efforts have been effective and significant. I can imagine her wondering if there will ever be true joy again. This is rubber-hits-the-road time. How does God give strength to these good people?

First, let me tell you about their kitchen. It's small, cozy, and recently remodeled to fit the size of their home now that the kids have gone off and had kids of their own. There are only two chairs at the kitchen table. On the table are some bottles of pills. Those of us past fifty know about those. And there also is a Bible and a daily devotional booklet, which is opened regularly under the light of a small table lamp. There is warmth and light in that small kitchen. The text from Isaiah comes to mind: "Morning by morning he wakens—wakens my ear to listen as those who are taught" (Isa. 50:4). Our friend is a fine teacher, and he knows how to sustain the weary with a word—because he himself knows what it is to be sustained by God's Word.

Finding God's strength usually means surrendering some of our need to be in control. It's helpful to do that before you're ready like Isaiah to say, "I quit." But God is patient and willing to hear your anger, your whining, and your pain. Look for God's activity when people are experiencing difficult times and calling on God. When we aren't so busy paddling upstream, we might begin to notice the subtle clues God is using to get our attention. Subtle things like a parishioner saying, "We just don't want to do that, Pastor" or attendance dropping off at the new country-western Christian rap service.

I've also experienced the presence of God when grief knocks the song right out of you. When my mother-in-law was killed in a car accident, my husband and I grew extremely weary. We were sad, and we were grieving, and we also were bone tired. In that place of weakness and grief, the prayers of our congregation lifted and carried us as surely as I carry newborn babies to the baptismal font. We were held in the arms of God in very real, tangible, and humbling ways. Looking back I wonder how we managed to keep going while driving back and forth to the hospital for several weeks. I've thought of times when pain like this can be so isolating and devastating. Yet we felt carried, supported, and strengthened by God's presence within and in the people who were "Jesus with skin on" in our sorrow. I've heard people recount over and over again that when they look back on times of crisis, they can see that God was there.

For Group Discussion and/or Personal Reflection

1. Think about difficult times in your life. In what or whom or how did you find strength in those times? Who were God's angels to you? (Who showed up and helped?) Were you aware at the time that God was present? Can you look back now and see that divine help might have been there even if you didn't see it at the time?

2. Have you ever had prayers for help answered? Have you shared that experience with someone else? Why or why not?

3. Have you ever asked God to take over, even for one day? What would that mean to you? How would you hear God's directions or find God's strength?

4. How would you translate into plain language these beautiful words from Handel's *Messiah,* inspired by Isaiah: "Come unto him all ye who labor and are heavy laden, and you will find rest, unto your souls"? What does it mean to "rest" your soul?

4

Hope for the Hopeless

"He was despised and rejected by others; a man of suffering and acquainted with infirmity; and as one from whom others hide their faces he was despised, and we held him of no account" (Isa. 53:3).

We're Not Alone in Our Suffering

Does it help you to know that Jesus experienced the full spectrum of human joy and pain? I find it helpful to consider that the worst possible thing we can do might be murder, and yet Jesus forgave even his murderers. He forgave those closest to him, who deserted him when he really needed them. Consider this example: "Then Jesus went with them to a place called Gethsemane; and he said to his disciples, 'Sit here while I go over there and pray.' He took with him Peter and the two sons of Zebedee, and began to be grieved and agitated. Then he said to them, 'I am deeply grieved, even to death; remain here, and stay awake with me.'" (Matt. 26:36-37). But of course, they didn't. Despised, rejected, agitated, grieving unto death—could that be finding life so unbearable that Jesus longed for death?

One of the most painful experiences we can endure is running out of hope—hope that the pain will go away, hope that we can beat the cancer, hope that tomorrow will be a better day, hope that our loved ones are safe. When people are hopeless, joy gets strangled. Then nothing good can fight through the darkness of despair. The world seems to revolve around our fear and pain. There's no room left for love, compassion for others, or for God. Hopeless means we have lost faith and feel alone in our fight against the giants.

Hopeless means the only thing we have to hold on to is holding on. And one of the things that intensifies the suffering is the feeling of being isolated and alone. Those are the moments when we feel like crying out as Jesus did out from the cross: "My God, my God, why have you forsaken me?" (Matt. 27:46).

There are situations when entire nations, like Israel captured and enslaved in Babylon, fall into despair and hopelessness. Corporate hopelessness like war, poverty, or catastrophe, usually needs a corporate response to help communities begin to regain hope. God cares about that. Think about how many times God addressed Israel the nation as opposed to specific individuals. Think how often Jesus focused on the nation, the group, the whole church. God's individual servants can pour out God's love, but never as powerfully as a united community focused on God's mission. (It takes a group to send help into situations like New Orleans after Hurricane Katrina.)

It would be easy to build a biblical case for the fact that the faithfulness of the congregation as a whole has as much importance to God as the lives of the individuals making up the body. Is your congregation hope-less or filled with hope? Do you trust God to lead? Do you reach out as a body? Do you make efforts to preserve unity within the body or are you casual about amputations and disease? Churches and individuals need to hear Paul's words to Timothy: "We have our hope set on the living God" (see 1 Tim. 4:7-10). Once we understand that anyone within our "body" who is suffering and hopeless is a priority for all of us, we're in a better place to consider individual hopelessness.

If my elbow, my knee, or even my pinky finger hurts, it becomes the center of my attention really fast. Yet, somehow it's easy for us in the body to send the message that emotional suffering like hopelessness needs to be kept out of sight. There's a suspicion that such a condition shows a lack of faith or maybe is even sinful. But how can that be? Didn't Jesus cry out, "My God, my God, why have you forsaken me?" Didn't he sweat blood in the Garden of Gethsemane?

So let's just accept, for better or worse, that prolonged pain of any kind may produce hopelessness. And sometimes hopelessness is motivation that sends us looking for the reality of God.

Conquering Fears

Now that we know that there's no place in the Bible that tells us to "mind our own business," let's talk about individual hopelessness. God cares about that, too. As society becomes increasingly complex and difficult, more and more people seem to be suffering from hopelessness, anxiety, fearfulness, and a lack of a moral center. Isn't it interesting that at the same time that hopelessness seems rampant, fewer and fewer people are seeking hope in the church?

Let's get really personal. Do you have trouble sleeping, eating, or relaxing? How's your neck? Are your shoulders tense? Do you regularly use antacids, alcohol, too much food, or other self-medicating drugs to outrun the fear that perhaps your life hasn't had much meaning and never will? What's happening that Americans are so anxious, that sleep disturbance is so common, and that life is such a struggle for so many of us?

I read somewhere that fear is the opposite of faith. But Scripture reminds us that "perfect love casts out fear" (1 John 4:18), and we should not "worry about anything" and instead "rejoice in the Lord always" (Phil 4:4, 6). But it's not that easy! We remind ourselves of faith's power by singing songs like, "God is our fortress, we will never be shaken," even while our stomachs churn and one eye is twitching uncontrollably. Look how evil shows up and is described in the Bible: liar, deceiver, accuser, and a prowling lion waiting to devour us—we are not alone in our suffering. We have a cheerleader right next to us chanting: "Hit 'em again, hit 'em again, harder, harder." After all, who wins when God loses? There are still demons that only Jesus can cast out. Depression is a demon that can devour us if we don't get help.

If you have the tendency to beat yourself up when you have negative emotions, it would be a good thing to study how many times Jesus was not happy. He wept when Lazarus died. He got angry with the moneychangers in the temple. He rebuked his faithful follower, Peter: "Get behind me, Satan!" (Matt. 16:23). And as he prayed in the Garden of Gethsemane, he asked God whether it was really necessary for him to be crucified. Jesus wasn't disobedient. These are not sins. We shouldn't let the accuser, the "evil one" use our discomfort against us to make us even more miserable.

What, however, does God do when we call upon the holy to deliver us from despair? Fear and depression are like a black curtain in our lives that prevents us from seeing God's light. It's at that point that the community of faith needs to surround people in pain until they can stand on their own feet. But it's difficult for the community to help if people in pain keep it to themselves. Because of the stigma of emotional difficulties, too many people go without help. We don't need to be afraid or ashamed to ask God and our community for healing. Many miserable Christians (oops, I mean Christians who are miserable!) need to be reminded that calling on medical and mental health professionals is no different than getting a cast for a broken leg. There's no burden we carry that God wouldn't be glad to lift from us!

A Case Study in Despair

The story of Jonah is a good case study in despair. First, he knew what God wanted him to do, and he rebelled and ran away. He tried to hide. He made a choice to ignore God. He soon found himself in deep trouble in ways I'm sure he never saw coming! Eventually in the belly of the whale (okay, big fish), he came to the conclusion that the only way out of his troubles was to give up his stubborn refusal to accept God's agenda and ask for help. But his heart was still not in the right place. He was desperate, but still unwilling or unable to forgive his enemies, the Ninevites. So even after the whale puked, Jonah was still in trouble. He wasn't yet praying, "God, grant me the serenity to accept the things I cannot change," or "Not my will, but your will be done." And he continued to struggle.

Jonah's view of justice and fair play did not include forgiving his enemies, the Ninevites. His heart was hard. When God forgave them, he rebelled once again. He wanted the world to go his way, not God's. His pride caused his downfall. God gave him comfort (a small shade plant). He felt a little better. A little relief is helpful when the tension level is very high. But then God burned up the plant to teach Jonah about himself. Jonah wanted to be in control. When the plant died Jonah was ready to die, too. He didn't want to live in a world that didn't play by his rules.

When we give up the idea that the world needs to play by our rules, we can sometimes trade in hopelessness for peace. Other times it's not that simple. But no matter where the darkness comes from, the Savior shines a light straight into our hearts and asks, "Do you want to get well?" You can be healed but not cured, emotionally comforted but not physically healed. You can be reminded as often as necessary that you are not alone. God can reach you, hold you, and give you hope in resurrection and change in this life or in the next. Everyone who walks in darkness is offered a great light. Sometimes our friends have to put us on a stretcher and lower us through the roof, dragging us to the source when we are no longer capable of getting there on our own. Sometimes our friends have to drag us, kicking and screaming.

The people who have walked in darkness often have powerful stories to tell about their experiences with the great light. "Arise, shine, for your light has come" takes on a whole new meaning for those who have been knocked down by life and have given up on positive change. God cares about them and Jesus waits for them—for us—with open arms. Healing often begins when we can pray, "nevertheless, not my will but yours be done" and place our lives in

God's safekeeping while we heal. Sooner or later when God calls on us to "go make disciples" we will have a story to tell about God's strength and power.

For Group Discussion and/or Personal Reflection

1. We often are given opportunities to reach out to others in combined efforts through the church. In what sorts of opportunities have you participated? How have you experienced the truth that it is more blessed to give than to receive? How did you or those on the receiving end feel God's presence?

2. What "random acts of kindness" do you practice in this increasingly mean-spirited world? If you don't usually do random kind acts, what holds you back?

3. Can you recall a time when you overcame a feeling of hopelessness? How do you believe God was involved? Who were the people that helped? Remember this exercise the next time you are feeling alone.

5

Redeem, Redeemer, Redemption

"The spirit of the Lord God is upon me, because the Lord has anointed me; he has sent me to bring good news to the oppressed, to bind up the brokenhearted, to proclaim liberty to the captives, and release to the prisoners; to proclaim the year of the Lord's favor, and the day of vengeance of our God; to comfort all who mourn" (Isa. 61:1-2).

God's Plan for Redemption

I have noticed that when you ask people to put religious language into their own words it's often very hard for them to do so. Grace and redemption are probably the hardest things to explain, especially if you haven't experienced them. The prophet's announcement that God would send someone to proclaim liberty to the captives and release to the prisoners is usually understood to mean people who are caught in "bondage to sin," if you don't mind a little more church language. Generally I understand these to be people who need redemption, because they have begun to think of themselves through the eyes of past mistakes and not through God's eyes.

You can't experience redemption unless you step into God's kingdom. Until you taste freedom you may not recognize when you're stuck. Redemption in this life is subtle, and it requires the ability to be self-reflective. I often see highly anxious people who have no idea why they are anxious or even that they are anxious. God can calm and encourage them, but first they have to see themselves as they really are. That's not always so easy. When I began flailing around for ways to explain grace and redemption I understood why Jesus told fourteen parables about "the kingdom of God."

I brought up the topic at dinner with my family, throwing a rather tense moment into an otherwise pleasant occasion. "So what do you think redemption means?" I asked my brother. Quiet descended around the table. But older brothers can never resist being the "teacher," so I knew I had him hooked. Eventually he said, "Everybody sells their souls sooner or later, the question is to which idol? What are you willing to do almost anything for? And then when the eventual dead end and broken dreams come, who or what can give you a second chance?" Hmmm. Not bad. But what does *he* know? He's Presbyterian. However, it's a good place to start. (I hate to admit that he *might* be right.)

Here is a definition of *redeemer* from *The New Student Study Bible* (NRSV, Augsburg Fortress, 1990): "One who frees or rescues another, especially from sin." Rescue from sin means easing or removing the consequences of our wrongdoing. Unfortunately redemption happens after the sin. If we cash it in before we sin, redemption turns into cheap grace. My daughter once did something she knew her dad wasn't going to like one bit. Actually I can't remember which time this was; it happened more than once. When I challenged her with her dad's inevitable response, she said, "He'll get over it." That's cheap grace, planned on in advance!

Where do we go when we have messed up so badly that we can't even make jokes? Who do we tell when we are ashamed and sad and in need of a second or sixtieth chance to live the way God wants us to live (for our own good and in God's goodness)? When are the times in your life when you wish you could hit "rewind" and take back the hurtful words or deeds that caused so much pain?

The prophet proclaims: "Do not fear, for you will not be ashamed; do not be discouraged, for you will not suffer disgrace; for you will forget the shame of your youth, and the disgrace of your widowhood you will remember no more. For your Maker is your husband, the Lord of hosts is his name; the Holy One of Israel is your Redeemer, the God of the whole earth he is called. For the Lord has called you like a wife forsaken and grieved in spirit, like the wife of a man's youth when she is cast off, says your God. . . . In overflowing wrath for a moment I hid my face from you, but with everlasting love I will have compassion on you, says the Lord, your Redeemer" (Isa. 54:4-6, 8).

God's promise is that the Savior would reach into the broken places of our lives—the broken hearts and the sense of worthlessness with which so many people live—and release "the captives." But how does this happen? What is redemption like? Here are several images about redemption, but not fourteen!

Green Stamps and Airline Miles

Here are two examples of redemption programs. Which one do you think is most like God's forgiveness? I have some silverware that looks rather like gold. (But all that glitters is not gold. You can tell because after thirty years the gold is flaking off.) My great aunt got it by saving Green Stamps and turning them in at the "redemption" center. It was a place where you turned in worthless stuff (little green pieces of paper) and got back something of much more value (silverware, Betty Crocker cookbooks). I can also redeem airline miles in our frequent flyer program. It's a valuable perk. Every time I fly I get points, and sooner or later I earn enough for a free trip.

Christians are often confused about which kind of redemption program God offers. Do we earn enough miles to travel into God's good grace and eternal reward? Or do we trust that when we turn up with the bits and pieces of our lives—little scraps of this and that—Christ will put it all aside, both the good and the bad, and say, "I have provided the free gift—all you have to do is sign in on the 'God's people' list and stay in touch with me. I'd rather think God just watches for those who are ready to be loved, rescued, or communicated with. Otherwise what hope is there for all the "lost sons"? With God, there are redemption opportunities available 24/7, but you do have to show up at the redemption center. God's forgiveness isn't automatic. Confession and a "contrite heart" come first.

Calling for Roadside Assistance

Many people live fearing that when trouble comes and we ask, "Can you hear me now?" no one will answer. However, imagine being given a cell phone that has unlimited minutes, no roaming charges, and free long distance. (I have given this gift to my college-age daughter and it seems now to be necessary for her survival.) There's a little instruction card with the phone for calling roadside assistance. We can use the card to dial 1-800-GOD-HELP. It's a collect call billed to Jesus. Upon dialing we receive an automated prompt: "If you are truly sorry, press 1. If you understand your error and realize you have a part in this trouble, press 2. If you would like forgiveness and a second chance and are ready to change so that you don't need to use this card again, press 3. If you are calling to blame someone else, please go back to the main menu to repeat these options. If you would like to speak to an operator, get down on your knees and please wait for assistance. Your call is important to us, please do not hang up."

When would you use this feature? Well, let's say you took a dangerous detour from God's road and you are now stuck in the ditch. Your wheels are spinning and you can't get out on your own power. Maybe you're lost, without a map, but you generally are not in the habit of asking for directions. You're in danger because you don't know that there's danger. We would do well to remember that Jesus can help, but we have to make the call.

Redemption happens like this: We pull the card out of our pocket and place the call. A tow truck shows up, kind of scruffy with beat-up lettering on the side that reads "Emmaus Road Service." The driver doesn't look much like an angel, but he leans out the window and says, "Got your call. Jesus sent me. The bill's already paid. Where would you like to go?" If we are smart we say, "Back to the Garden, or anywhere where love is freely given and received and God is on our side." After all, isn't that paradise? When our hearts and lives need repair, whether they are "totaled" or just badly smashed up, it takes a leap of faith, a posture of humility, an honest look, and the sorrow of accepting our own responsibility (confession) before we can experience the true value of the servant's work as Redeemer.

What's Your Idol of Choice?

We need redemption. We need forgiveness. We need help. When people are really stuck, they may realize for the first time how much they need God. It's very sad how broken we allow ourselves to become before we are ready to change and accept help.

What's your idol of choice? What would you sell your soul for? Material success? Someone who loves you the way you think you need to be loved? Your children's future happiness? Power in the company, or in your community? Toys? More vacation time? Less time with your spouse? (The origin, I'm told, of ice fishing—for both men and women.)

What are you willing to risk everything for? Whatever the apple that evil holds up to us, it is usually not easy to dismiss. Support for new priorities and change is necessary. You need both divine help and a group of people who can help encourage you. God created the church not just to serve others, but to help us remember and tell each other, "I am in bondage to sin and I cannot free myself. I have turned my life over to God. Please give me the courage and commitment not to grab it back as soon as I feel discomfort, fear, or pain."

If we are going to follow a living God we have to admit our brokenness—we are cracked pots, imperfect vessels willing to be recycled with God's love and reshaped by God's servant. Our role is to sit in Christ's living water to be filled up and spilled over to others. Lo and behold, while we are serving and pouring we also realize that we are being mended-glued back together and recycled for a new future.

For Group Discussion and/or Personal Reflection

Here's a list of what God promised the Messiah would do:

- Help others see and believe that God is real and present. Share God's wisdom, love, and truth in community.
- Strengthen the weary by equipping us with the power of the Holy Spirit and a mandate to go out to the world in his name.
- Provide hope for the hopeless, the final hope being life after death.
- Redeem us in God's eyes, release us from the things that bring more death than life, and assure us that when "God looks at us, he just sees Jesus." This is the promise of God's free pardon for now and eternity.

With this list in mind, search your life or your world for places where the Risen Christ in the form of the Holy Spirit is at work. Pray for faith, trust, and eyes to see where God has been at work. And consider these questions:

1. Where or when have you seen these activities going on? How about in your life?

2. Do you believe that God promises faithful servants will be protected from suffering, blessed with wealth, ensured of worldly success, or are exempt from following the Ten Commandments?

Can you find evidence of this in Scripture? Can you find evidence for the fact that God's priorities might have changed in the last few centuries?

3. Can you think of things Jesus said or did that could *not* fit broadly under one of the above four categories? (Sometimes Jesus demonstrated to us that God strengthened him, etc.) Make your case biblically and discuss it with your group, if you are participating in one.

Part Two

Our Response to God

God's plan for all of us:
to become a mature participant
in the body of Christ.
We grow when we stay connected
to Jesus, the vine.

Being connected to the vine is a practice
that eventually becomes a habit.
Like being married, it's a set of habits that becomes an identity.
Like marriage it's a relationship that takes commitment.
It takes courage to make this kind of commitment.

Perfect love casts out fear, if you let it.

6

Transformed by the Spirit

"That you may know that it is I, the Lord, the God of Israel, who call you by your name. For the sake of my servant Jacob and Israel my chosen, I call you by your name, I surname you, though you do not know me. I am the Lord, and there is no other; besides me there is no god" (Isa. 45:3-5).

The Potter's Work

God wants a relationship with us. God longs to etch this knowledge on our hearts: "I am your God. I call you by name." When we believe that, we can begin to trust. When we devote our best selves to God, it's the beginning of wisdom. When we surrender our broken selves, it's the beginning of transformation. When we give our lives to God, it's the beginning of peace. That's God's truth.

God wants us to know the truth, to obey, trust, and let God be God. According to the prophet Isaiah, "Does the clay say to the one who fashions it, 'What are you making'? or 'Your work has no handles'?" (Isa. 45:9). Not if the clay knows what it's doing! Rather, it is our place to say, "Yet, O Lord, you are our Father; we are the clay, and you are our potter; we are the work of your hand" (Isa. 64:8).

How does God "lay hands on us" as the old gospel hymn goes? God really does change lives, but only lives that place themselves like clay at the potter's disposal. This process of being changed say from a butter dish to serving platter or even a work of art, is through a lifestyle of submitting to the shaping work of God's Holy Spirit. The bottom line is that God transforms us through what we call "faith practices." These practices—really just a description of the way the Holy Spirit has access to our hearts—are both ancient and true. Once you recognize them you can see them woven through the life that Jesus led and modeled for the disciples. You can see them woven into all of Scripture. Read through words to hymns in the Trust, Guidance or Commitment, Discipleship sections of our *Evangelical Lutheran Worship*, and you may read with new eyes!

It is the Holy Spirit, promised to the disciples at Pentecost, who works to transform us. When the Spirit is present, the fruits of the Spirit begin to be visible in our lives. It's all connected. In the pattern and the produce we see God's holy purposes for the world. The general plan for all of us is to be part of that purpose. Consider the hymn, "Come, Holy Ghost, Our Souls Inspire" (yes, I believe in ghosts—at least this one!):

> Come, Holy Ghost, our souls inspire.
> And lighten with celestial fire;
> Thou the anointing Spirit art,
> Who dost thy sev'n-fold gifts impart.
> (*Lutheran Book of Worship* 473)

God's specific plan for each of us is to shape us into the likeness of Christ. You can see in many places in Scripture and in many hymns the request for daily guidance, transformation, and help with obedience and trust. One of my favorite hymns sums it up nicely:

> Spirit of God, descend upon my heart;
> Wean it from earth, through all its pulses move;
> Stoop to my weakness, strength to me impart,
> And make me love you as I ought to love. (*ELW* 800)

The writer goes on to ask that God "take the dimness of my soul away" (reveal truth), "let me seek you and, oh, let me find" (experience builds trust), and "teach me to love you as your angels love . . . my heart an altar, and your love the flame." Our hymns are filled with words such as, "Breathe on me, breath of God, until my heart is pure" *LBW* 488) that describe a process Christians have understood since the disciples began speaking in foreign languages on the day of Pentecost. The Holy Spirit continues to strengthen and equip us for the servant's work. When that happens our strongest witness is the transformation of our priorities. Jesus continues, through us, to show people that God's power and God are real.

The Gifts of the Spirit

God sent the Holy Spirit to a select few in the Old Testament. Only the called and chosen received the Spirit's gifts. Solomon, for example, received the gift of wisdom. Samson received supernatural strength. The prophets received—you guessed it—the gift of prophecy. But without help, the people were slowly crushed with their inability to obey God's laws. Then God "poured the Spirit" into Jesus. I can't begin to sort out when, where, and how Jesus and God were one, but I trust that Jesus sent access to the Holy Spirit for all who trust and obey God, beginning with the dramatic display at Pentecost, when Peter addressed the crowd, quoting the prophet Joel: "In the last days it will be, God declares, that I will pour out my Spirit upon all flesh, and your sons and your daughters shall prophesy, and your young men shall see visions, and your old men shall dream dreams. Even upon my slaves, both men and women, in those days I will pour out my Spirit; and they shall prophesy" (Acts 2:17-18).

Everyone has access to the gifts of the Spirit, through Jesus. This was an absolutely new development to the listeners in Jerusalem that day. For many of us, it may be also. The gifts of the Spirit transform lives. Transformed lives will continue the work we inherited as followers of Jesus Christ!

There are at least seven faith practices: prayer, worship, service, witness, sacrifice, study, and encouraging others. Through these seven "avenues," if not more, we open ourselves to God's transforming power. When we spend time with God, it changes us. Those changes are visible in the fruits of the Spirit. They are: "love, joy, peace, patience, kindness, generosity, faithfulness, gentleness, and self-control" (Gal. 5:22).

It seems to me that the fruits of the Spirit are evidence of God's spirit within us, just as spiritual gifts are equipment from God for mission in the world. If we are not convinced of God's reality and God's wisdom, we aren't going to be very willing to share it. If we try to serve God or others by our own strength, we are vessels that will soon be empty. If we have no hope, we can hardly point to the hope that we have. And finally if we have never experienced the freedom and release that's described with words like God's forgiveness, redemption, new life, grace, and mercy, we won't have much to share except sympathy when we see other people make mistakes that could cripple them for life and eternal life.

We have to see God at work in our own lives before we can talk about it with passion. Jesus prayed for the disciples when he was leaving them, that they would stay connected to the source of passion, strength, and purpose and not fall away from God. Connection to the source happens through a lifestyle of faith practices. Let's see how that works!

For Group Discussion and/or Personal Reflection

1. If faith practices are like ingredients to making a cake, which ingredients do you run out of most frequently: prayer, worship, studying God's Word, giving, serving, encouraging other believers, or sharing your faith? What prevents you from making that (or these) a habit? How can you re-prioritize your days to include what you might be lacking?

2. If God's purpose for your life is to transform you into the image of Christ, how is it going so far? Each one of us has specific road-blocks to faith and specific temptations. Can you identify yours? Ask God to help remove them.

3. If God's plan for your life is that other people can see God's power at work in you, in what ways could your faith be more public without being pushy?

7

Guard the Treasure

"Hold to the standard of sound teaching that you have heard from me, in the faith and love that are in Christ Jesus. Guard the good treasure entrusted to you, with the help of the Holy Spirit living in us" (2 Tim. 1:13-14).

"Not My Will but Thine Be Done"

I read recently that true freedom is getting over the need to insist on having our own way. Love, we are told in Corinthians, doesn't insist on its own way. God is love and doesn't insist either. But God encourages us to taste the freedom of living without fear. God's peace comes to us through trust. So many songs about the peace of submission come to mind, like the old Gospel hymn: "Have thine own way, Lord, have thine own way. Thou art the potter. I am the clay. Mold me and make me. . . ."

Sunday was a stewardship Sunday for us. I had been thinking about trust and obedience so my sermon was easy to write. It was about submission. I dug up an old hymn (at least old by the standards of our contemporary worship service). The title was, "I Surrender All." Something happened during the hymn that touched me deeply. A quiet hush fell upon the congregation and then they began singing in parts. It was beautiful, reverent, trust-filled singing. It was as though through their voices they were giving themselves over to God. I have to admit I don't hear that kind of reverence often displayed. We understand submission, but we often forget about it.

Submission means surrendering our will to do God's will when the two are at odds. In a world where almost all authority is questioned, how does the word *obedience* sound in your ears? Submission, surrender, and obedience—these are not things that the word *grace* erases like so much writing on a chalkboard.

Over the years I have had several small dogs in obedience training and they all flunked miserably. The reason? I had mixed feelings about obedience, even for them. Did I want them to come, sit, or stay because they were afraid or because they were hoping to get treats from me? I discovered that dogs, like people, no matter how small they are struggle for control. They want to be the alpha dog or the leader of the pack. Until they are willing to let you be the alpha dog, obedience is a real struggle.

The beginning of a healthy relationship with dogs is to establish both trust and boundaries. God probably finds us as hard to wrestle with as I did trying to wrestle with a creature that weighed about fifteen pounds. You want to give freedom, or it isn't a fair fight and it's not love freely given. You don't want to swat them. (Well, you do sometimes, but you restrain yourself so that they won't be afraid of you the next time.) You don't want to scare them to death for they will develop fear responses for the rest of their lives. You also don't want to crush their spirits. I personally don't like dogs or people who are all slobber and no spunk. God doesn't want us to give up strength, healthy pride, the use of our intelligence and willpower—but God does want us to know that we are second (Beta) and God is both Alpha and Omega (the beginning and the end of life).

I hope my analogy doesn't offend you. Sometimes we don't trust God because we are afraid to give in to rather unhealthy ideas about obedience and surrender. We are created in the image of God, after all. And God said that people, the world, and all creation are "good." I don't believe that Jesus tries to control our behavior with threats. But I believe that for our own good, being "outside" God's "box" is dangerous. As soon as we start thinking that we are exempt from obedience we are in trouble.

I don't want to call us dogs. It's not a very nice image for a lot of people. Jesus called us sheep though, and I can tell you if you've ever seen sheep it's much less flattering than being called a dog. There are times when we need shepherding. If we don't allow it, we wander into dangerous territory where we can no longer hear or care about the master's voice. When excess pride or fear shows up, we are truly in danger of being lost. And like men with a map in their hands who refuse to seek help, it can be humorous or tragic.

Does obedience mean ignoring all of our God-given faculties, strengths, and gifts? Or is God rather nudging us along to be as whole and mature as we can be? What is true for human relationships is also true for our relationship with God. If a parent or a partner is over-functioning and making all the choices, the child or under-functioning adult becomes dependent and rather helpless. As a parent, I want my daughters to use their gifts and continue to grow in confidence, both in themselves and in God. I can't force them to do things my way now that they are young adults. If we have been good parents, we haven't been forcing them or controlling them with fear. I don't believe that God uses force or threats to control us either. The power that God has in our lives is like the power an adult child gives to a parent who has earned trust through consistent and wise loving.

God inspires, breathes strength into us, and sends servants to support us when we are weary. God will carry our burdens, soothe our fears, and quiet our hearts. Even adults need that. But God allows us dignity. We can refuse. We can make choices. We can be afraid to trust. We can insist on our own way. We often do. It's like a twist on the popular wall art poem: Some days looking back over my path in life I see two sets of footprints in the sand. Then there are times when the footprints change and only one set is visible. "Why is that, Lord?" I ask. And God replies, "Those are the days you took the bus."

Training Us to Live in Relationship

"You then, my child, be strong in the grace that is in Christ Jesus; and what you have heard from me through many witnesses entrust to faithful people who will be able to teach others as well. Share in suffering like a good soldier of Christ Jesus. No one serving in the army gets entangled in everyday affairs; the soldier's aim is to please the enlisting officer. And in the case of an athlete, no one is crowned without competing according to the rules" (2 Tim. 2:1-5).

Good soldiers go through basic training. "Basic" is pretty physical and from all reports not a whole lot of fun. Christians-in-training are not promised that discipline will always be a lot of fun either. We are enlightened or taught the truth, given faith practices to allow the Holy Spirit to work within us, and then sent into the world on a mission that would seem impossible, unless you have faith.

What is our training regimen? Our youngest daughter just started college track training. She is motivated to do well. She trains with the team three hours a day. She watches her diet. She knows how much sleep she needs. She'll ask the trainers for help with an ankle that gives her trouble. The training and discipline are paying off. She's already faster this year than she was in her fastest time last year. Her clothes are starting to fit differently. She's being outwardly reshaped by the discipline.

Christian disciplines reshape our inner lives. Our coach is the Holy Spirit who pulls up alongside of us and gives us words of encouragement or correction. Some people call these experiences "God sightings." I like the term. It reminds me that God is at work in my life and, when I am attuned to the Spirit's nudging, I can continue to be transformed. Let me give you some examples.

"Can I Get a Witness?"

While writing this book there was a period of time when suddenly I just fell silent. (Believe me this is unusual!) I sensed that there was something more I needed to know or see about God's power and presence. I suspect I just fell into a time of doubt. This is very normal and predictable for all of us, maybe especially so if you are getting ready to lay your faith out on the line for inspection. My prayer for several days had been, "Teach me about your power, God. Use me as your witness. And could you hurry up—I'm on a deadline here!" It was then that our daughter, Emily, invited me to go with her to church.

Emily doesn't attend an ELCA church. She attends a campus church sponsored by The Assemblies of God. But she is an active, faithful Christian, and she is an adult and can make her own choices. Because I wanted to be open to God's invitation and because I love my daughter very much, I agreed to go. But I admit I was prepared to be uncomfortable and underwhelmed. My first observation was that the church was filled with an endangered species: young people worshiping God. My second observation was that the photographs that lined the walls, arranged like stations of the cross in a Catholic church, were all of people hugging, helping, serving, and laughing with other people. Their bulletin announced a short mission statement: "Love God, love people. Period."

Emily told me that the service would be longer than ours. I noticed a Starbucks coffee counter in the back, so I was prepared. The service began with about a half hour of singing, sprinkled with only a few words here and there. She called the singing, "the worship time." I thought the whole thing was "the worship time," but this wasn't a time for questions. Pretty soon I was totally into the music and forgot about my reservations and the fact that the pastor looked like a biker and drove a Harley.

Next came the sermon about, you guessed it, the work of the Holy Spirit and spiritual gifts. I admit to a certain amount of Lutheran pastor's envy. The sermon was thirty minutes long and people were taking notes! Clearly I was dreaming. The sermon was well done, no red flags from me on the playing field. But then people were invited to come forward if they would like to receive spiritual gifts, any gift that God cared to give them. What followed was about thirty minutes of almost the entire congregation coming forward for prayer from a prayer team. The comment that sticks with me was the pastor's remark, "We are not here to talk about God. We are here to experience God doing something right here, tonight, in your lives."

I wanted, honestly, to go forward and just get a closer look. But I seemed to have Lutheran lead in my shoes. So I went back to the coffeepot and watched how comfortable people were praying with and for each other. I browsed in the books-for-sale shelves, retreating to thinking about God. I bought a book and stayed as far to the back of the church as possible. Just because I wanted to know about it, didn't necessarily mean I wanted to experience it—with other people, or now, that is. "Maybe later, God," I thought.

I went home and read the book. It was all about demonstrations of the Spirit at work, and the visibility of spiritual gifts (not artistic natural talent but prophesy, healing, and other things that aren't genetically transmitted). I was way out of my comfort zone, but did remember having asked God to "show me." So I prayed, "God, I believe you are loving, transforming, and that you help me daily in ministry, but something's going on here that I don't get. Am I too dumb to understand this or don't you trust me or what? Is this you, from you? You're going to have to show me something more, Lord." I did sound a bit like Thomas to myself and winced.

This is an absolutely true account. The next day while I was at my office, a man with twinkling eyes, scruffy beard, and rather crumpled clothes—I'm guessing a logger or a mechanic—came into the church. I was there alone. He asked if there was a pastor available. (I'm used to this. It's okay.) I told him who I was and he asked, "Can we talk a minute?" The short version is that he had been medically "dead" from a heart attack and the doctors revived him. While dead he had had a conversation with God about his unfinished business. (I'm just using his language, reporting what I heard.) He wasn't much of a church-goer, but thought of himself as a believer. Now he prayed every morning and was starting to read the Bible. He told God that he wanted to express gratitude. So he pulled out a check and said he was going to give $1,000 dollars apiece to four churches in town, asking that we use it to help the local community. Clearly this was not given out of abundance.

I thought it would be impolite to take the money and run, so I asked as casually as possible, "So, what was it like to be dead?"

He smiled and replied, "Well, I didn't really want to come back because it was so inviting. But it wasn't my time."

Of course we can only say that in faith we accept the answers to prayer. We can never really prove faith to each other. We can only say, "Through eyes of faith this is what I saw." God answered my prayer, and much faster than I had expected. In fact, I was in shock and didn't say anything about it for a few days. I had to ponder it in my heart.

For Group Discussion and/or Personal Reflection

1. Reflect on times when you believe that God answered prayer or "touched down" in your life. You may have to think carefully. Looking back, when has God seemed closest and most near to you? What were your faith habits at that time?

2. When has God seemed farthest away? What were your faith habits at that time?

3. What is the state of your training regimen? Begin praying for God to increase your trust and for opportunities for you to "risk" trust. Make notes about your prayer. Don't give up!

8

Prayer, Witness, Worship, and Study: Avenues for the Spirit

"These are the things you must insist on and teach. Let no one despise your youth, but set the believers an example in speech and conduct, in love, in faith, in purity. . . . Give attention to the public reading of scripture, to exhorting, to teaching. Do not neglect the gift that is in you. . . . Put these things into practice, devote yourself to them, so that all may see your progress" (1 Tim. 4:11-15).

"First of all, then, I urge that supplications, prayers, intercessions, and thanksgivings be made for everyone . . . so that we may lead a quiet and peaceable life in all godliness and dignity" (1 Tim. 2:1-2).

The Witness of Obedience

I have talked a lot about the importance of obedience to God and trusting the potter to transform us into vessels that can hold the Spirit's gifts. Now I'd like to venture into how those gifts, poured into us, can be poured out for one another.

Some faith practices help change us inwardly; some help us encourage others with our obedience. They are part of God's plan to let faith "be caught" by seeing it alive in others. Over and over again Paul told his apprentice to pay attention to his own discipline: "Put these things into practice. Devote yourself to them, so that all may see your progress" (1 Tim. 4:15).

We need a lifestyle of opportunities to let the Spirit "build up the body" as well as our own trust. Faith has always been alien in culture and opposite our human natures. We need each other for support and encouragement. We need to look for God not only working within us, but also working among us. Together we are God's people. Alone we are only prodigals and easy picking for hungry lions, demons, and fortune hunters.

The Sacrifice of Worship

Worship, like giving, is a sacrifice first and foremost. God commanded worship way back in the Ten Commandments. Maybe it's for our "Sabbath rest" or maybe it's for God's benefit (bring your sacrifices to the altar). But it doesn't say anywhere in Scripture that regular worship is only for those who feel like it. We are not the audience in worship; we are active participants. We bring our worship, devotion, and sacrifices to God. But instead of bringing our spotless lambs, first child, or grain from the harvest, Jesus says, "Stop. I have already made the sacrifice. Go in peace. And serve the Lord."

Worship encourages others. Worship unites us in song, in prayer, and in creed. Worship blesses us as we kneel confessing our sins and seeking honest connection with each other and with God. Community teaches us the truth about ourselves. What we do is always more true than what we say. Do you love God? Feed my sheep, said Jesus. Do you love your neighbor? Invest in encouraging their faith. Walk the second mile, forgive seventy times seven, don't be that voice that divides the "body" with gossip and complaint.

The first motivation for worship is always, "Remember the Sabbath to keep it holy." It starts with obedience, with kneeling at the throne saying, "I am here, my Lord, at your service." How the gift of worship is wrapped or presented probably doesn't matter all that much. What matters is our motivation. There's no magic formula for sincere, true worship that will please God. A high church mass or a tent revival in Mississippi may both be sweet incense to our Lord. Worship is about devotion. That means devoting our attention and time to God. We can worship without ceasing as well as pray without ceasing when we just keep an attitude of awareness, gratitude, and the desire to be obedient in our hearts. Sacrifice means willingness to suffer. You can't take suffering out of the equation of Christian obedience. It may be a little thing like giving up "your seat" in worship, or "your music" in worship, or "your comfort" in worship. It might even be surrendering the attitude that says worship is for you. Or it might be really taking up your cross.

Worship gives us a place to invite people to see God's power. If nothing else those gathered in worship have been inspired to get up and show up. If you want someone to "come and see" those who love the Lord, where else would you invite them? Would you invite them to join you in the woods or at the ocean to delight in God's handiwork? Beauty awes us, but it doesn't transform us. I love being quiet in the woods, but if I didn't know the Bible I wouldn't have a clue about the "still small voice" and what it might be saying to me. I crave experiences by the ocean. But I never come back from the ocean thinking about my sin, or my neighbor's need, or the congregation of people who I serve and love.

The Witness of God's Word

I've experienced the chaos in congregational life when the Bible is no longer considered our guiding truth. I've had a church leader tell me that "I know that's the Christian thing to do, I just don't feel like doing it." Bottom line? He wasn't willing to let the Bible have any authority in his life. When you know what God wants and you deliberately choose to do the opposite, I think we can clearly say, "Jesus is not Lord," for you at that moment.

Even as I say that, I know that there are those who will ask, "Well, how are you using the Bible? How do you apply it? Do you believe it's literal?" Of course there are many things we could talk about when we say that we believe in "the authority of Scripture." For me, it's like having a bad connection on my cell phone: If I stay on the line long enough I will get the big picture the other person is trying to convey, even though the details may be a bit fuzzy. There are some parts of Scripture that are so obvious, repeated so often, so central, that unless we just feel like being cantankerous there's not much to debate.

Christ's mission is pretty clear. He summed it up in the Great Commission, sending the disciples out into the world to be servants of the Servant. Still we can lose our way. When the congregation that I serve became serious about evangelism and outreach, typical of most congregations in this process, we experienced rather heated conflict. The more people who were anxious about change, the more heated and inflexible they became. Rational discussion gave way to comments like, "I don't care about other people, I just care about the people who are already here." People were grumbling, secret meetings were held, some people started leaving, and the leaders in the church asked, "Is this really necessary?" So we brought in some help. She led us through discussions about what it means to be a "faithful church." Initially the council members were restless because we started with Bible study. They wanted to know what to do about what they perceived to be "alligators" and crisis. They wanted her to tell them what to do.

She patiently and calmly led us through Scripture about the mission of the church, what Jesus said to the disciples about their mission, and the activities of the early church. Some of those who were reluctant to endure conflict over the changes, now understood that being faithful meant "taking up our cross." They were ready to let the Bible have "authority," and to let "Jesus be Lord." Otherwise whoever makes the most noise wins, and that's usually not God!

The Importance of Prayer

People who pray regularly are probably those most capable of being clear about God's answers to prayer and what God is doing in their lives and in the lives of those for whom they pray. If you don't ask, how do you know there's an answer? These are quiet, private things. But they have deep and lasting impact on our faith and our personal lives. Transformation begins when our inner dialog (you know, those thoughts we usually don't speak out loud, and sometimes for good reasons?) starts to be shaped into thoughts that Jesus would approve of. Our inner lives can torment us or bless us. We can be putting on a happy face, or a smart face, or a proud face on the outside while cringing in fear and sadness on the inside. We can be doing all the right things and feeling resentful and hateful—the old "do-the-right-thing-for-the-wrong-reasons" routine. First and foremost, God wants to grow "integrity" within us. That means to integrate what we believe into who we are. Praying is an attitude of receptiveness to the influence of God's wisdom and love. Even when we aren't talking, we can be praying (without ceasing!).

I remember reading a spiritual maturity chart that went something like this: Kindergarten prayer: "Give Me"; Adolescent prayer: "Help Me"; Mature prayer: "Use me." Now, all of us have childish moments and selfish moments and moments when as adults we really need help. But when we get to the awareness that prayer is often about guidance, and faith is about "going," we have crossed some invisible line into committed discipleship.

Many Christians understand prayer as the time when the whole group joins in the Lord's Prayer, or the family joins in the four-second "Come, Lord Jesus" table grace. Any ritual can be richly full or as shallow as a lake in a drought area; it just depends on the inner condition of our hearts. That's why our private relationship is so crucial for the foundation of our corporate life together. When Jesus is *really* Lord, then we know that praying for others is a discipline of the heart growing from and for compassion. It's not a chore to ask

God to bless people when we love them, no matter how long it takes. Once you are convinced that prayer does call on the Holy Spirit and that many voices are stronger than is a single petition—when the community prays in faith—it's more than a roll call for the sick. We pray expecting God to move, to respond, to touch.

How good it would be if we also reported all the answered prayers in the community! That's a powerful witness to the Spirit at work. I love it when we get cards and letters thanking us for the prayers of the church. Some include words like, "And I could feel the strength of your prayers." Others report that unexpected healing and deliverance has happened. And some just say, "Thanks be to God!" We're all on a journey. If we are "faith" full we expect God to hear and answer. Most of us have a little room for more trust in the power of prayer. Trust is a habit that grows with repetition.

For Group Discussion and/or Personal Reflection

1. What are your current faith habits or practices? Do you experience them growing your desire and ability to be in relationship with God?

2. Do you experience God's Spirit when you worship? How do you prepare your heart for worship? What do you come to worship expecting? Are you communicating to God or observing while in worship?

3. What is your private communication with God like? Some people say that the most important thing we ever do is pray. Why do you think that's true or untrue?

9

Service and Sacrifice: Opportunities to See God's Power

"For the grace of God *has appeared,* bringing salvation to all, *training us* to renounce impiety and worldly passions, and in the present age *to live lives* that are *self-controlled, upright, and godly,* while we wait for the blessed hope and the manifestation of the glory of our great God and Savior, Jesus Christ. He it is who gave himself for us that *he might redeem* us from all iniquity and *purify for himself* a people of his own who are zealous for good deeds" (Titus 2:11-14, emphasis added).

My computer doesn't like the way Paul writes. I don't much either. But I have highlighted the important words in the above passage in case they get lost in abstraction. The point is Christ came to create a "people" that would be God's people, servants and witnesses.

Jesus gave his disciples commands that I believe we continue to receive today. "Come, follow me." "Go, and make disciples." "Be my witnesses to the ends of the earth." "Keep this new commandment: Love one another as I have loved you." "Remember me." "Teach." They didn't always get it right. Neither do we. Jesus sometimes complained and didn't exactly say, "Good job!" But when the seventy came back rejoicing that they were in fact being used by God to heal and cast out demons, he rejoiced with them.

We are sent into service, the work of Jesus Christ, while we are still in training. There is no graduation from the sanctification process in this lifetime. The disciples were serving before Jesus was crucified. As they served they began to see God's love flowing through them. The result of their service was not as important as the trust in God's power they could see while they were serving. You can't separate service from trust, or trust from obedience, but without the whole we will never see the fruits of faith.

Listening for Christ's Command

How do we continue to hear Jesus or the Holy Spirit speaking to us? We say "hear," but very few people mean hearing audibly. Somehow it's hearing within your heart. (Although I have met people who claim to have heard audible words.) In our hearts the words seem to jump out like little arrows from Scripture, in prayer, in speech from another person, and the arrows seem to hit dead center to the needs of our souls.

Sometimes God uses sign language. That is when we read the message through the events we see going on in our lives. Again, we accept the messages in faith, enlightened by what we have learned about the Holy Spirit and its work. Jesus said the Spirit would call to mind his teaching and his words. First they have to be entered into the "memory" of our data banks. That's why it's so sad that so few people know Scripture. I know this story from the book of Acts:

"Now there was a disciple in Damascus named Ananias. The Lord said to him in a vision, 'Ananias.' He answered 'Here I am, Lord.' The Lord said to him, 'Get up and go to the street called Straight, and at the house of Judas look for a man of Tarsus named Saul. At this moment he is praying, and he has seen in a vision a man named Ananias come in and lay his hands on him so that he might regain his sight'" (Acts 9:10).

Remember the man who came to visit me after I had worshiped at my daughter's church? It was sort of like that visit by Ananias. You'd think I would have been happy at such a quick response to my prayer for direction. But I was a little disappointed. "Now what?" I thought (and prayed). I began to sift through everything I knew about the Holy Spirit. And while I did this, the face of a man at church came to mind. He's a pastor. I don't know him well. I believe that he's charismatic. I know that he uses a different religious vocabulary than I do. I also know that he is what I call a "prayer warrior"—someone who prays a lot and believes in answered prayer. His name popped into my head for several days. Not being completely dense about how God gets my attention, I finally decided to call him.

I said, "I don't really know how to start this conversation, but I think God wants me to talk with you. Feel free to humor me. I am out of my comfort zone here." Although he worships with us fairly often, I had never really talked with this man before. There was a long pause at the end of the line. Then he said, "Now I want to tell you something. I've been praying for months that God would give me an opportunity to talk with you about the kind of power Jesus has. But I decided if God wanted that to happen I would let you initiate it."

We met, talked, prayed together and I got goose bumps when he gave thanks for a "miracle." I thought, "Hmmm." I guess when God arranges events and does it in a response to prayer it *is* a miracle. I thought they would be more dramatic somehow. Maybe that's why we so often overlook them.

Lazarus at the Gate

Jesus told a story about a beggar named Lazarus, who sat at a gate and was passed by many times by a rich man. When Lazarus died, he went to heaven, and the rich man went to hell. The rich man looked up to heaven and saw Lazarus and asked for help. But no help came. (You can find the story in Luke 16.)

I'll tell you my real life Lazarus story. Recently I was in Mexico with our daughters. While shopping for the best bargains we could find on silver jewelry and trinkets, we passed a tiny, old woman wearing a blue bandana. She held out her small, wrinkled brown hand and mumbled one word in Spanish. I walked past. After all, I don't speak Spanish. And I wanted to make it home in time to go to the fiesta. However, my daughter stopped, put a coin in the woman's hand and gave me an inquisitive look. "Busted," I thought. My excuse was that my daughter understood her and I didn't. But I did.

The next day I saw the same tiny, grizzled old lady again. This time she was standing across the street from where we were taking the bus. Our bus was coming and I only had a moment to respond. I missed the moment. That night I had a vivid dream. It was unpleasant. In the dream I saw the face of the tiny, old woman with the blue bandana on her head. Somehow it disturbed my sleep.

The third day, farther on down the street I walked out of a corner grocery and almost stepped on the same tiny lady with the blue bandana. She looked at me and didn't even hold out her hand. But did I dig in my purse? You bet. Have I ever noticed the same person on the street three times when I've been in Mexico before? Never.

Where is God in this story? I don't think the lady was poor, bent over, and shamed into begging just so that I could come along and learn a lesson. I don't think that God planned she would grow old and die in poverty. But I do believe that God's Spirit worked within me to show me God's truth and open my eyes to the need of my neighbors. The strong have the responsibility to take care of the weak. The poor, who will always be with us, give us the opportunity to outgrow greed, fear, and lack of compassion. They give us the opportunity to demonstrate God's love. God used her poverty to touch my heart. God opened my eyes to see poverty in a new light. It was an opportunity for me to practice trust and obedience. It was an opportunity for service and sacrifice.

I have seen poverty many times, but this time I came home deeply burdened by all the poverty I saw in Mexico. I'm not sure how God will use that yet. But I know that seeds of some kind were planted or watered. That's how God leads, grows, and nudges us into service born out of obedience. It may not be a burning bush. It may just be a simple moment, a simple request, and being awake enough to see with enough faith to believe. The Spirit whispered, "Lord, when did we see you hungry?"

I am not always listening. I am not always willing to be obedient. God's not done with me yet. But I do see that the more I desire to be obedient, the more I see God at work all around me. I also "hear" and "see" many more opportunities to trust and risk obedience and serve God.

For Group Discussion and/or Personal Reflection

1. What makes it difficult for you to trust God enough to risk obedience? What keeps you from a life of service in God's name?

2. How have you experienced God "nudging" or "correcting" or getting your attention through the Holy Spirit? Have you ever told anyone about it? Why not?

3. Can you think of a time in your own life that reminds you of a time from Scripture?

4. When have you have acted on something you read in the Bible, such as, "Just as you did it to one of the least of these . . . you did it to me" (Matt. 25:40)? Are there times when passages from the Bible or Christian songs pop into your head and seem very appropriate? Jesus said the "Counselor" would remind us of his words. First we have to have heard or read them. What are your study habits?

Part Three

God's Love Moves through Us

God's plan is general:
Creating a people who live in holy relationship and peace.

God's plan is also individual:
Helping each of us give and receive love in a community
that unites to serve, train, and send new servants into the world.

It's not about you. And it's not just about God.
It's about community. That's the bigger picture.
It's always in community that we find our purpose, our place,
our deepest joys, and enduring significance.
It's only in the Body that we are whole.
It's only in Christ's mission that the Spirit shows us
the purpose, power, and presence of God's gifts.

Where two or three are gathered,
we find out who we really are,
and why we need God.

10

The Body in Motion

"You then, my child, be strong in the grace that is in Christ Jesus; and what you have heard from me through many witnesses entrust to faithful people who will be able to teach others as well. . . . In a large house there are utensils not only of gold and silver but also of wood and clay, some for special use, some for ordinary. All who cleanse themselves of the things I have mentioned will become special utensils, dedicated and useful to the owner of the house, ready for every good work. Shun youthful passions and pursue righteousness, faith, love, and peace, along with those who call on the Lord from a pure heart" (2 Tim. 2:1-3, 20-22).

We Are the Church, the Body of Our Lord

God's purpose for each of us is to grow and develop our unique, God-given gifts in order to make the world a better place, to strengthen our relationships, and to make our communities whole. This happens when all people use their gifts cooperatively for transcendent purposes. God nudges us toward opportunities, counsels us against detours into darkness, and rescues us when we fall away from our place in the community. We are not meant to live alone. We only know ourselves honestly when we see ourselves interacting with others. We only know our need for God honestly when we see ourselves interacting with others. It's always in the community that we find our place, our purpose, and our deepest joys, and sometimes our deepest hurts. It's in community that the Spirit shows us the purpose, presence, and power of God's gifts.

The Church is a mission outpost where the Spirit calls us, shapes, delights, and transforms us into servants of the Servant.

Then we are sent out, instructed to love the wolves, be witnesses to what we've seen and heard, and avoid taking the credit for God's success. Transformed people, living obediently and quietly without the contagious striving of our time, fear of failure, or desire for worldly power, are truly miracles among us. When we've seen their faithfulness, we can only point to God and say, "Thanks be to God!" or "Praise the Lord!" Then we might dance like David danced or sing like Miriam sang or even understand raucous praise music!

I have met many people who call themselves Christian the way my husband might call himself "Swedish." (His mother was born and raised in Sweden, but he wasn't.) There are a lot of good-hearted, generous, kind, and civic-minded pagans. Some of my best friends are pagans. I love pagans. They never let me forget that I need to be able to articulate my faith. But believing that God exists and serving God are about as different as knowing the ice on the now frozen lake will hold you and driving on it with a pick-up truck.

Christianity is a lifestyle, not an idea. And it's a lifestyle for communities.

I have never met a practicing Christian who doesn't need a faith community to challenge, support, encourage, strengthen, and outreach, and just plain live with. I have never seen individuals powerful enough on their own to be a continuous pressure on the culture for justice and compassion. I have never seen governments able to enforce the Ten Commandments. I have never seen people changed by guilt, fear, or reward. Only the love of Christ experienced through the Body of Christ can implement that kind of change. God's purpose isn't about "me." It's about "we."

Understanding Motivation

We need to pray for eyes to see and ears to hear God's truth and the truth about ourselves. What would motivate us to risk change? Those who work in a field called "change management" study things like motivation. Daryl R. Conner, author of *Leading at the Edge of Chaos* and *Managing at the Speed of Change,* says we do know what motivates individuals and corporations to risk change. Here's a list paraphrased from *Leading at the Edge of Chaos* (New York: Villard Books, 1989). The motivations are ranked from most to least effective:

1. Pain is the most effective change motivator: If the platform we are standing on is on fire, we are highly motivated to jump off.

2. Fear is the second strongest motivator: We will change to avoid negative outcomes.

3. Working toward an extraordinary goal with many perceived benefits is third: It's like the carrot and stick routine.

Do you see the implications for the church? Looking at motivations 1 and 2, it's easier but not more comfortable to understand why some churches preach hellfire and damnation so successfully. Lutherans, on the other hand, have most often focused on grace and the hope that people will be motivated by gratitude to follow God. Unfortunately, gratitude for gifts does not necessarily lead to transformation. Ask parents giving gifts to children at Christmas! They always want *more!* That's why I don't pull punches when I say "the church as we know it is in trouble." I believe the church, universally, has not made a compelling enough case for Christianity in recent years because we have become so comfortable that we forgot we needed to. Lutherans who initially used the church to preserve their immigrant identity were so focused on preserving the past, they forgot to develop outreach tools for the folks who don't eat lefse.

What will motivate the church to change its practices? In a world where people are struggling with doubt about the existence of God, pleasing God is not a high priority. It hurts me to see many people who find faith to be just one more consumer product to help them feel better. I am afraid for the next generation who may not have enough passionate Christians who can pass on the faith to them. I'm afraid that mainline churches will miss the opportunity to speak from our perspective because we haven't spoken a language that today's culture understands. So there are some primary motivators that have helped me become passionate about evangelism! And the place to start, for all of us, is with our own relationship to God. I am hardly a "witness" if I haven't guarded the treasure that has been entrusted to me.

The unchurched and the de-churched and even the churched need us to talk about what God is doing in our lives. If we witness from our own experience, people who trust us may begin to trust God. People who already trust God may be encouraged to witness to others. We need to stop being private about our faith!

A Word to the Church

Whenever we begin to think that just finding the truth in a book or a person or pure doctrine is all we need, just think about how many really smart people are arrogant, mean, or just plain nuts. Whenever we begin to think that all we need to do is the right thing at the right time, think about how really difficult it is to sort out the difference between want and need, God's will and our own near-sighted greed.

When God's people are squabbling about power like James and John, or busy enforcing rules like the Pharisees, or reaching out without looking in, those peeking in the windows become disillusioned. They don't want what we have. They can't tell we are Christians. They don't see the saints, only the sinners. Without submission, trust, or walking humbly with God, our lives are the same as pagans, misfits, or cultural snobs.

But when the church's one foundation is really Christ the Lord and when hearts are changed and we can give our neighbor love, living together respectfully, responsibly, with perfect love casting out our fear, then the world can be saved from the evil we produce when we only serve ourselves.

Then we can trust, obey, and serve the one who loves us whole and well. And the Holy Spirit that transforms us and sends us out to tell, sends us peace, blessing, strength, and hope, saying: "Beloved servant, you've done well."

For Group Discussion and/or Personal Reflection

1. What would motivate you to risk change in your faith life? What do you think needs change or growth?

2. What would you like God to change within you? Have you asked? Has God answered?

3. How would you describe your participation in your faith community? How would you describe your congregation's expectations for sharing faith together? How do you welcome or reach out to unchurched people?

4. What would you say to friends and family members who might be curious about your faith?

11

Detours and Distractions

"There is one body and one Spirit, just as you were called to the one hope of your calling, one Lord, one faith, one baptism, one God and Father of all, who is above all and through all and in all.

"But each of us was given grace according to the measure of Christ's gift. Therefore it is said, 'When he ascended on high he made captivity itself a captive; he gave gifts to his people.'

"The gifts he gave were that some would be apostles, some prophets, some evangelists, some pastors and teachers, to equip the saints for the work of ministry, for building up the body of Christ, until all of us come to the unity of the faith and of the knowledge of the Son of God, to maturity, to the measure of the full stature of Christ (Eph. 4:4-8, 11-13).

It seems that life should go more smoothly than it does. God has some priorities; maybe you could even call them a "mission statement." Jesus gave it to us. God's people are called, loved, and given gifts for the journey. We have a basket of gifts from the Spirit to share with the world. We can ask for more. So what goes wrong?

Paul wrote to the Philippians: "Not that I have already . . . reached the goal; but I press on to make it my own, because Christ Jesus has made me his own. . . . I press on toward the goal for the prize of the heavenly call of God in Christ Jesus" (Phil. 3:12, 14). Like Paul, we see the goal and head off in the direction of it. But unfortunately, we get distracted along the way, like little Red Riding Hood and her basket of goodies, and pretty soon it's common that we start listening to the wrong voices and taking detours.

Affluence

One of the detours leads us down the path of affluence. Along this path, we begin to devalue the fruits of the Spirit we carry in our baskets. We might even trade them in for plastic imitations. I've been wondering what crippled the churches in Europe. (I refuse to admit that they can't be resurrected!) My husband, who has spent much more time there than I have, thinks it was just affluence. When there's no need to give to the church to keep the doors open, the practice of sacrifice is forgotten. When the standard of living is so high because the government takes care of the poor, the exercise of compassion isn't as necessary perhaps. Health care, college tuition, and living expenses more in line with salaries means people are less aware of human need. Is it really so difficult for rich people to get their Volvos through the eye of a needle? Jesus thought so. Do you have to be poor to see your need for God? Or does affluence numb us into ignoring the pain just beneath the surface?

While we're busy trying to reach those mountain peaks where the "haves" look out in serenity (or apathy) at the "have nots," perhaps we should pause and consider one possible benefit of the media's obsession with stars who have fallen from their pedestals. Clearly we can see that the very rich and famous can be just as unhappy as the very poor and unknown. Loneliness and addictions cut across all levels of income and success. You don't have to follow the lives of many politicians, sports heroes, media stars, or multi-millionaires to see that money and worldly success don't buy happiness.

The rest of us who aren't rich and famous (the majority of us) are busy trying to find the "American dream" in the midst of diminishing financial security and increased workloads. We have our own dangers; maybe believing the myths that enjoying life can wait until retirement or we can turn back the clock on our aging bodies. It doesn't have to be like this. We do have choices. You may not be willing to "downsize" for a better quality of life, but many of us do have that choice.

Distractions: Crises or Opportunities?

It's all about perception. I have never appreciated when in the midst of pain or difficulties someone reminds me that every crisis is also an opportunity. What they mean is, if the platform is on fire it's an opportunity to make a change. "Oh, joy. Send me more opportunities," is not usually the first thing on my mind. But sometimes the only way God can get our attention is by allowing this kind of opportunity. Jesus, Paul said, learned obedience through suffering. When we call out to God, God is there and we know it, even if the pain persists. It is often suffering that drives us to our need for change.

Paul writes: "And not only that, but we also boast in our sufferings, knowing that suffering produces endurance, and endurance produces character, and character produces hope, and hope does not disappoint us, because God's love has been poured into our hearts through the Holy Spirit that has been given to us" (Rom. 5:3-5).

Sometimes people give up on God, saying, "How can God let these terrible things happen?" I wonder if God is also asking, "How can they let these terrible things happen?" God gets blamed for some of our mistakes. I also wonder if there were no suffering in the world what opportunity would there be for us to learn compassion? What would draw us out of ourselves if the poor were not always with us?

Local Brush Fires

Conflict in churches is a major distraction. In one church parlor where I worked there was an elegantly cross-stitched wall hanging that read: "Where two or three are gathered in my name there will be conflict. —Jesus." That's probably fairly correct.

Jesus and his disciples disagreed. The early disciples disagreed. The early churches disagreed. Christians continue to disagree. It's normal. How we disagree is the question. It's an opportunity, not a crisis unless we make it a crisis. What does learning to resolve conflict peaceably teach us? The most important skills for relationships are peacemaking and compromise. Conflicts, great or small, are opportunities to let God teach us how to speak the truth in love. This is a skill that would greatly increase peace on earth!

Look at it like this: Does someone upset you? Do you try and work it out or run for cover? Do you "demonize" them behind their backs, or do you risk speaking the truth (as you see it) and risk hearing the truth (as they see it)? Christian living takes courage.

Does someone hurt you? They aren't sorry? What does it mean to forgive seventy times seventy? Do you look for your contribution to the problem or only try to insist on your solution?

The body of Christ is a place to learn about cooperation, forgiveness, compromise, and grace. It's a place to learn to get over our fear of difference and learn to love even our enemies for Jesus' sake. We can't do this without the help of the Spirit. The only way to get over our "animal" instincts is to replace them with our "God" instincts. This takes heavenly help and practice. It doesn't come naturally.

For Group Discussion and/or Personal Reflection

1. Most of us have good intentions. What are the things that distract you from continuing to practice faith if you are a believer?

2. Are you living by a set of ideas or priorities that really don't match up with following Christ? For example: Is work more important to you than your family or your faith?

3. If you have ever strayed from the faith, dropping out for lack of interest, time, crisis, or doubt? What brought you back?

4. What does it mean for affluent, comfortable people to let "Jesus be Lord?" Why does this seem so difficult?

12

The Plan: Gathered, Equipped, and Sent

"Jesus said to them, 'While I was still with you, I told you that everything written about me in the Law of Moses, the Books of the Prophets, and in the Psalms had to happen.' Then he helped them understand the Scriptures. He told them: the Scriptures . . . say that all people of every nation must be told in my name to turn to God, in order to be forgiven. So beginning in Jerusalem, you must tell everything that has happened. I will send you the one my Father has promised, but you must stay in the city until you are given power from heaven" (Luke 24:44-49 CEV).

I'm a baby boomer. I'm not a good committee person. I'm often tempted to give up on institutions, including the church. But then I see God at work there doing so much more than I could ever expect or hope to do on my own. God reminds me over and over again, "It's not about you. It's about us." Sometimes when the "thinkers" lose their way, the good hearted, the God-hearted call us back. Sometimes when the leaders lose their courage, the faithful speak words of encouragement. Sometimes when "me" seems so much more important than preserving the "we," I see how God can work among us so much more clearly than I can see God working through me. Sometimes when denominations are busy trying to get their ducks lined up, the church communities are already swimming across the river, leaving the leaders well behind.

Where do I see God? Where have I seen God? Where have I experienced God's love? Predominantly through God's people—as imperfect as we all are—in the church. I have seen the servants of the Servant carrying on the work. I have recognized the tracks of the Holy Spirit more times than I can count and many more times than I've talked about. So let me close with some stories about God working through ordinary folks in congregations. Let me tell you some of the ways I've seen God pour love through clay pots. We don't always hear the "good stuff."

A Cloud of Witnesses

I have met children who have never been to church. I have met adults who have never been to church. It's hard for me to think about the things reported at evangelism conferences, such as on the East and West coasts it's typical for children to now be three generations away from a relative who practiced faith. It's hard for me to hear my daughter report that she can't find a single church holding services—Protestant or Catholic—in the town of fifty thousand in Spain where she is spending the year. How will they know about God unless someone tells them? How will they understand faith if no one teaches them? So I am grateful for the many Sunday school teachers and influential role models who God used to help me come to believe that God is real.

I've met many pastors along the way in my rather nomadic life whose sermons helped me grow in faith and understanding. I remember the pastor in my seventh grade Presbyterian confirmation class who told me that I wrote beautiful prayers. I remember the Southern Baptist who somehow talked me into being "dunked" after already being through two other baptisms. I remember the college chaplain who asked me to preach in chapel (before women were being ordained in the Lutheran church). I remember his comment that if the seminary ever allowed women I should head there. I remember my mother's devotions with us at the dinner table and bedtime prayers when she sat on the side of the bed and listened and encouraged. I remember hearing Handel's *Messiah* for the first time in sixth grade when our church choir sang it. I thought the angels themselves were singing. I remember how the church gathered around my family when my mother died. I know that part of the deep ache I felt after her death was eased by loving people in congregations. I was a part of many after she died. For better or for worse they became my family. I don't know how people come to faith without the church. Clearly we see that in America right now, they don't.

Lutheran Voices

I like the idea that the Lutheran Voices series that this little book is part of is a chorus of Lutheran "witnesses" from around our denomination. While writing this, I decided to add some back-up singers to my efforts. You'll recall how I invited people from my congregation to gather around my kitchen table over the summer and discuss the topics of this book. It was a wonderful gathering of saints.

I asked them to tell me their stories about the people and experiences that helped them believe God was real. I heard stories about relatives who modeled faith both by visibly demonstrating faith practices and talking about faith with them. I heard about the grandma who taught that "everyone is beautiful in God's eyes" and started the first school for mentally handicapped children. I heard about family traditions of remembering the "Sabbath." I heard about adult siblings sensing God's strength and power when they gathered to keep watch with their mother as she died. Normally not emotionally close, they found themselves holding hands and singing hymns for their mother, attracting the attention of and probably witnessing to the nursing staff in the hospital.

There were many, many stories of answered prayer, role models, congregational influence, and the impact a good friend who can talk about faith can have in your life. Those who prayed regularly for others on our prayer chain commented that this practice grew compassion for others within them. They begin to think that perhaps they were getting more than they were giving, by taking daily requests for prayer from people in need.

When my husband and I go on vacation we've discovered the power of having congregational members preach. We've done this for several years now. We also ask a graduating senior each year to preach on Mother's Day. (I can't think of anything that would make a Christian mom prouder than hearing her child talk about a living faith!) Every time we ask a lay member to preach, we have to spend time helping them prepare to risk something new. That's natural. But the fact that people are willing to accept our invitation shows the Spirit at work. In another denomination they would probably call this "testimony," and it's a powerfully moving witness.

This year our high school principal talked about growing in faith during his struggle with cancer. He had always been a practicing Christian, but the depth of this experience transformed his faith, his priorities, and his outlook on life. He found strength and a new hunger for a relationship with God. His prayer life became more regular and more intimate. He didn't know which psalm it was, but he prayed, "The Lord is my shepherd" a whole lot. He was very clear "that he didn't want to be thought of as some sort of faith hero," but he wanted us to know how the power of our prayers and his struggle had brought him to a deeper walk with God. We laughed with him about his self-consciousness. Most people are very hesitant to talk about their faith. Many people told him, "Boy, I could never do that!" But the truth is they will remember his story for a long time. Because they respect him, it was a powerful witness. The fact that he would accept the challenge is also a strong witness to God's ability to strengthen and equip his servants.

Instruments of God's Strength

God often sends servants to hold us up when the legs get knocked out from underneath us. When life knocks the song out of your life, a healthy congregation will sing for you—in words and prayers and even hot meals (don't underestimate the healing power of a good hot dish!). The body of Christ at work has the fullness of God's power behind it. Our prayer chains get requests for prayer from places way beyond our county lines. Over the years it isn't unusual to hear people who have been prayed for say, "I could feel the strength of your prayers."

God works through people who are motivated to pour out God's love. But God also comes to us directly. Before we can pour it out, we have to have a little bit in our hearts to pour out. That's why we need to at least be in a process of inner transformation, before we get too heavily engaged in God's mission. If God's not working with us and through us, our efforts will be commendable perhaps, but not remarkable. Alone we are not the "body of Christ"—we are maybe just a pinky finger. We have to try and team up with God, not just ask God to cheer for us.

There are many times when I have felt God use me. These are times when I've been really aware that I needed to get out of the way and just trust God to show me what to do. They usually involve some fear and risk. My reaction when it's over is usually gratitude and awe. Whenever I reflect on God's strength, a particular time always comes to mind: I got a call late one night from a local policeman who's a member of our congregation. He said, "Pastor, there's a women here who's asking for you to come. You don't know her, but she visited our church one Christmas Eve and evidently was impressed with you. She doesn't have a church. Here's the deal: her teenage daughter just found the husband dead in the woods. He shot himself. It's pretty bad. I think she's in shock. Could you come?"

Of course I said yes. But I've gotta tell you I was shaking in my boots. I started arguing with God as soon as I hung up the phone.

"God, you know what a soft heart I have. I'm just going to cry and how will that help? Lord, I have a weak stomach. If I have to see the body I'm not going to be very pastoral. Dear Jesus, what can I say?" By the time I got in my car my prayers were barely coherent. Pretty much just, "Help. I don't have a clue what to do." I think I also reminded God, "Okay, here I go, but you better come with me because that woman needs more than I've got to give." I call it the "beg-and-bribe" sort of praying.

When I arrived, there were police cars all over the place. It was a dark, long country driveway back in the woods. With my headlights, I could see the man I knew waving me in to a place where I could park. I lowered my window, and he said, "We have to make room to get the body out. We'll be doing that fairly soon, Pastor." I gulped and proceeded to park and walk with him to the back steps. I don't remember what he said while we walked. I remember a deep quiet and calm I never expected. The woman and her daughter were sobbing in the corner. The male cops were standing by looking helpless.

The woman got up to greet me, saying, "Oh, thank you for coming. I was at your . . ." and I just threw my arms around her and she began to sob. Pretty soon the teenage daughter was also wrapped around us sobbing. The man who had called me gave me the thumbs up sign. Later he told me that that's what he wanted to do, but he didn't feel that he could or should. She didn't need me to talk. She just needed to know that somewhere there was a strength she could lean on because hers had just given out. Amazingly I didn't cry—well, not much anyway. I didn't start shaking until I was home safe and it was all over. You might call it an adrenaline rush, but I know it was more than that. I felt a hand on my shoulder and a strength much greater than my own. God's love was pouring through me, cracks and all.

Many of the people gathered around my table in the summer could tell stories about trusting God's presence to help them through whatever storms they encountered. We decided we couldn't believe that God sent the suffering, but God certainly was present and responsive when we called out for strength, courage, and comfort. I have learned the most powerful lessons about God's faithfulness in crisis, but I would never say that God sent the crisis in order to teach me.

Vessels of God's Hope

It is a wonderful thing to be used by God to bring hope. It changes us more than it changes those who receive our help. We send out mission teams every year. They are made up of youth and adults from our congregation. They are sent to people who really need concrete, physical work and help. These "servant trips" change lives. The kids who go and endure hardship to bring assistance to flood victims in New Orleans, drought victims in Africa, poverty victims in America, and older people with no resources to care for their basic needs, never forget it. Could an individual make it happen? Not unless they were very rich and had a lot of friends. It takes a congregation to be the "hands of Christ" to people in need.

These trips have generated many very moving stories. Hundreds of teens and their sponsors gathered from different churches all over America, come together for one week where they share worship and prayer, sleep on hard floors, shower with buckets or not at all, and work like slaves. And they love it.

One of my favorite stories is from New Orleans this past summer. The kids had no idea what they were getting into when they signed up for this one! Even a year later most of the areas looked like the disaster had only been days or weeks ago. People were living in cars, looking for bodies of loved ones, about as heartbroken as people could be. Our quilters at church sent quilts along for the kids to give away. Each student was given the "mission" to find someone to whom they wanted to give a quilt. They were to present the quilt, wrap it around the person's shoulders, and speak a word of comfort "from God"— basically to pray for them.

All the work groups stayed in one large church where the camp was set up. Three cooks were brought in every day to prepare meals for the teams. The first of our teams to present quilts decided to give theirs to the cooks. They were beaten down, older African American women who were incredibly gracious with this army of energy and noise! Several of the adults stood by when the girls placed the quilts around the shoulders of these women. According to my husband's eyewitness account, what came out of these kids when they prayed sounded like words straight from God's heart. Everyone cried.

A bit later my husband went back to the kitchen for another cup of coffee. The three cooks were standing in a corner, hugging the quilts to their chests and sobbing. There's no question that they felt the love of God through the hands of these kids from Northern Wisconsin. No one gets tired of this story. It humbles us all.

When quilts or prayer shawls are wrapped around shoulders, or strangers pull together in an effort to help other strangers, the Spirit of Christ reminds us, "Whatever you do to the least of these, you do to me." If God didn't call us together, unite us and call us toward a higher purpose, filling us with the desire to serve in Jesus' name, I'm not convinced that as many people would trust that God exists and is still visible working through and among us in our world.

Recently I attended a "Women of Faith" conference in Minneapolis. It's a gathering for women to hear wonderful, inspiring music and to encourage each other in faith. At one point a famous Christian singer asked us all to hold up our cell phones and turn the lights on, waving them while we sang. It's amazing to sing with eighteen thousand women. It's amazing to see so many little lights waving in a dark stadium. I wondered if the sound in that place was anything like angels in heaven around the throne of the Holy. Nothing has encouraged me as much in quite awhile as to see eighteen thousand believers "shine their lights." I've been to football games and baseball games in stadiums, but I've never had a sense of connection and strength there. It's more an "ant in the universe" feeling. But knowing that we were united by our belief and joined in worship was a powerful experience. There were people there from many states, many denominations, and many ages. Hope comes sometimes by remembering and seeing that God is at work in a whole lot of people. There is strength in numbers. It's the strength of feeling connected. It's the reassurance that if you are a fool for Christ, at least you aren't the only one.

Second Chances, Redemption, and Grace

Finally, although it's easy to talk about the times when God has seemed closest, when people have been witnesses, when we've received strength or hope or have been used in God's service, redemption is a different deal. Redemption stories are about as personal as spiritual experiences can be. You have to get stuck before you can get freed. Who wants to talk about getting stuck? People that can tell dramatic "change my life" kinds of stories point to pasts that are painful to share with others. Although, most have had vulnerable moments when we certainly know our own sin, describing them seems dull compared to dramatic conversions like Paul, or born again Christians, or addicts getting clean with the help of a higher power. Lutheran stories are often pretty tame stuff compared to that. "Well I was baptized at First Lutheran in Sioux Falls and . . ." You know how they go. However, most of us have moments when we realize we have been "released" or healed from some wound or sorrow. It may have been a slow process with no dramatic date for the calendar. One day we just notice that we're no longer bitter toward someone who has caused us pain for years. Or, after months of mourning the death of someone we love, we wake up one morning and gladly greet the day ahead of us.

We are now the servants of the Servant, a collection of clay pots in all sizes and shapes, formed by the loving hand of God for God's purposes. We can be filled to the brim with God's love. It pours into and through us to reach others. And other people pour out God's love to us. When we gather, the Spirit is with us, and when we go out, the Spirit moves with us.

I was reminded again last night of how powerful it is when God's people gather. Twenty of us held hands in a cozy room and prayed together. We had just discussed loneliness, isolation, and how many people feel cut off from each other and from God. It was particularly clear because we had just passed around a sheet of paper on which they were to list one friend they might invite to our next Bible study. Most of them couldn't come up with a name. We looked at each other with different eyes. In this gathering, in this moment, I experienced a quick recognition: this is God's purpose and plan—that all of us can hold hands and pray together in the name of Jesus Christ. And when we leave this circle, the strength of this community walks with us. God is at work in our lives. Thanks be to God! My prayer for all of you is that you find a circle where you gather and live, love and grow gathered around Jesus the Lord, amazed by his power and humbled by his love.

For Group Discussion and/or Personal Reflection

1. Do you have memories about being "released from guilt or sin"?

2. Are you carrying things on your heart now that have been heavy to carry for a very long time? Sit down in a quiet place and ask God to lift those loads. Ask for forgiveness and trust and belief in your "newness of life." Remember this prayer when you take communion the next time.

3. What would you like most to happen in your relationship with God now? Make some notes about how that could happen. Talk to God about it. Talk to a group or a friend who can help support you to take the time to make these changes in your routine. Pray without ceasing! Feel your heart expand! If you haven't already, read the book of Acts and find out more about the power of the Holy Spirit. Finally, just pray, and wait. Pray for wisdom, strength, hope, and forgiveness. And ask God to help you believe that your prayers are heard and answered, in Jesus' name. Amen.

For Further Reading

Personal Faith Growth

Foster, Richard J. *Celebration of Discipline: The Path to Spiritual Growth*. San Francisco: Harper San Francisco, 1978.

Kallestad, Walter. *Everyday, Anytime, Guide to Prayer*. Minneapolis: Augsburg Fortress, 1995.

Melander, Rochelle, and Harold Eppley. *Our Lives Are Not Our Own: Saying "Yes" to God*. Minneapolis: Augsburg Fortress, 2003.

Mowchan, Carolyn, and Damian Vraniak. *Connecting with God in a Disconnected World: A Guide for Spiritual Growth and Renewal*. Minneapolis: Augsburg Fortress, 2003.

Peterson, Eugene H. *A Long Obedience in the Same Direction: Discipleship in an Instant Society*, 2nd Edition. Downers Grove, Ill.: InterVarsity Press, 2000.

Yancey, Philip. *Church: Why Bother? My Personal Pilgrimage*. Grand Rapids, Mich.: Zondervan, 1998.

Congregational Faith Practices

Ackerman, John. *Listening to God: Spiritual Formation in Congregations*. Herndon, Va.: The Alban Institute, 2001.

Foss, Michael W. *Power Surge: Six Marks of Discipleship for a Changing Church*. Minneapolis: Fortress Press, 2001.

Groff, Kent Ira. *The Soul of Tomorrow's Church: Weaving Spiritual Practice in Ministry Together*. Nashville: The Upper Room, 2000.

Hanson, Handt. *Mission Driven Worship: Helping Your Changing Church Celebrate God*. Colorado Springs: Group Publishing, 2001.

Poling-Goldenne, David, with Shannon L. Jung. *Discovering Hope: Building Vitality in Rural Congregations.* Minneapolis: Augsburg Fortress, 2001

Theology

Allen, Diogenes. *The Traces of God in a Frequently Hostile World.* Cambridge, Mass.: Cowley publications, 1981.

Sponheim, Paul R, editor. *A Primer on Prayer.* Minneapolis: Fortress Press, 1988.

Other Helpful Resources

The Alpha Course: www.Alpha.com.

The New Testament, especially the Book of Acts.

Appendix:
God's Priorities at a Glance

"I will be your God and you will be my people"

	God gives the power of the Spirit only to:	The Spirit's power is used for:
Old Testament Period	Chosen servants Prophets Priests	Demonstrating God's reality Building faith communities Communicating God's desires Equipping servants
New Testament Period	Jesus	Demonstrating God's reality Building faith communities Communicating God's desires Equipping servants
Early Church to the Present	All believers who are dedicated to the mission (Matt. 28:19)	For the same purpose it has always been given: For demonstrating God's reality (God's justice, power, and wisdom) For building faith communities eager to do good works and preach the gospel

God's Priorities and Message:
1. Justice
2. Strength for Living
3. Hope in Suffering
4. Forgiveness through Jesus
5. Promise of Eternal Life

Other books in the Lutheran Voices series

Other books in the Lutheran Voices series

See www.lutheranvoices.com